what are words worth
Gaza is burning

Published in Great Britain in 2025
by Big White Shed, Morecambe, Lancashire
www.bigwhiteshed.co.uk
Printed and bound by Imprint Digital, Devon, UK

ISBN 978-1-915021-47-2
Copyright © Individual authors and artists
Cover Design by www.mollybland.co.uk
Illustrations by Calliope, Jane Wignall & Marett Troostwyk

A CIP catalogue record of this book is available
from the British Library.

Introduction

Why am I making this book? Because all I know is making books and sharing words, and because I don't know what else to do.

Thanks to all of you who have contributed and helped make it happen, to those who messaged to say they have no words right now, to those who are protesting publicly, to those who are having difficult conversations privately, to those who are sharing content and updates.

I would like to offer special thanks to Ambrose Musiyiwa for extending the call-out to his contacts, to Rosemary Drescher for her support with proof reading, and Molly Bland for her patience in producing the cover design. Everyone involved in this book has very generously donated their time and resources.

I asked for words of peace, hope, even rage, and that's some of what you will find in these pages. The breadth of voices and styles in this collection is staggering and I am very pleased to have been able to include artwork too.

Thanks to those of you who buy this book, your generosity has given us a place to share our feelings, and an opportunity to raise funds for humanitarian aid to Gaza. Proceeds from book sales will be donated to organisations specifically working to bring relief in Gaza.

The title is lifted straight from the lyrics of Tom Tom Club's 1981 hit, *Wordy Rappinghood* (give it a listen) and the headlines in the media on September 16th 'Gaza is burning' as Israel launched its ground assault.

Anne Holloway
Big White Shed

Marett Troostwyk

Contents

How Does the Moon Look from Palestine?

How does the moon look from Palestine?
Does a yellow crescent glow like it does here?
Will the little girl sitting amongst the rubble
Look up in awe as I do?
A momentary bubble.
Will we both hold our breath
To really feel
Its stillness?

Do the stars shine bright over Westbank?
Does the man, smoking his hookah pipe
Gaze up into the darkness,
As I do?
Does he think about how he is made from light and dust,
As I am?

And does the soldier in Gaza examine the constellations,
Thinking about stories of creation?
Grateful for a distraction from the harsh reality,
Our hearts hurting with every beat.

I can feel them
Through the land,
On the wind.
I feel their anger,
Hear their wails of despair.
I taste their tears in the rain,
And their love meets my love
In this cold night's sky,
As the moon slowly wanes.

Anna Greensted-Payne

I Can Confirm

that the sun still shines in a warzone
and that when it rains
(because rain, inevitably)
the ground still smells of heat after rain

the ground can shift
(because ground, inevitably)
still   hearts   beat

Is there a way back to you?
Sometimes permanence seems
the locative feature of loss.
Sometimes even under
asphalt, rock, layers of hard-packed history and hurt
a seed slumbers, waiting for this rain.

Mary Loveday

The Air

The air tastes different here,
When the blood is infused
With serotonin, the face
Already holds the terror
Of the moments passed.
Like the opening of the Trojan
Horse, like you rising
From your knee, diamond
In hand, them with hand
Still naked.
The air is not the same
When my son runs from the house
As a Chinook helicopter
Chuka chuka chukas
Overhead.
I wonder if in Palestine
There are still boys with walnut
Hair and coffee irises
With the naivety to run
Binocular eyes, heart imploding
With euphoria
Screaming: Mommy
A plane
A plane
A –

Casey Bailey

Bueno Comida, Bueno Compania

(good food, good company)

Today has a feeling of bubbling hot
So get some rice, get some chicken, bubble up the pot

And if you're asking about my aura
I'd say it's slightly complex

So if I work so efficient, and handouts we'll dish them

In a room full of creeds it's the difference that's intermittent

As to whatever was written, that isn't the shape of you,
but what you put into practice will impact shaping you

Now add your chopped up identity making it a full body
and you'll see the beauty in the mixture of the cooking pot anatomy

Unidentified flyness creating all types of culinary

Set the table, set the plates, set the bar for humanity,
making the thick jus of what you get from your family

Now let's have a feel at this craft of audacity

And remain with tha facts of the crisis for humanity

Richerprioritys

Nocturne for Gaza

On this strange night
flames leap into dark,
midnight-tinged, smokey,
reach for an open sky
fierce red licks, orange core,
intense and burning bright,
a backdrop to fireworks, bombs,
shooting stars as they fire
across the universe, marking death,

the television says twelve o'clock,
attacks imminent, sleep interrupted,
dreams of peace smothered. Alarms
and children cry for help,
they want to touch us, reach out,
but at this hour a heavy veil exists,
a space-age curtain obscures reality -
into frightened brown eyes, heat-seared,
we know we have failed you.

Gail Webb

Prayer for Peace

May every bullet become
a rose on hitting target

May drones sprinkle
petals of myriad flowers

May tanks dig furrows
planting seeds sprouting food

May bombs drop protection nets
over babies, toddlers, mothers and more.

May every bomb explode with healing light
magically restoring ruins to what they were

If AI can do it virtually
why should the material world lag behind?

Meher Pestonji

Elegy for a Palestinian Child

To be a dot on a page,
a breathless mark on white,
where ink forgets the warmth of hands—
such is the fate of the small.

Kites rise from tiny graves,
their tails tangled in smoke,
and the sky forgets to open
for the laughter that once flew.

The immortality of angels—
a tale buried in ancient dust.
Now, only sirens sing lullabies,
and tyranny plays the tune of noon.

The world shouts,
yet no ear bends to listen.
To exist no more than a name
scribbled on a schoolbook,
half-erased by grief.

To envy the butterfly—
its freedom, its colours,
its right to die
beneath a sun
and not a missile.

The tar spills from hearts,
to feel the ache of existence,
blackness clinging to fate's cruel hand—
to be a child is to not be,
a fleeting breath caught in time's grasp.
To envy the butterfly—
its soft wings brushing the wind,
its effortless dance beneath the sun,
a dance denied to those who are bound,
to those who are buried alive,
crushed beneath the weight of sorrow.

All of being,
the limbs of longing,
to be a grave—
the earth's cold embrace,
a body swallowed by its own silence,
perhaps it is the only way to rest.

Önder Çakırtaş

Serrata

Hunger (not mine), yet sense it –
a folded ache, a body closing in
                              on itself
like prayer mats abandoned mid-ritual.

I read until my jaw tightens, until
the rage slides down into my belly,
          where it stays, unscreamed.

There is no righteous anger in this.
No clean arc of resistance,
no speech held up like a shield.

Facing the act of stripping someone of breath, of face,
of name – the slow erasure called "necessary".

I watch the enemy speaking of precision
while children carry children in fragments.
Recognition does not rise from rubble – only silence does.
Dust coughed up in a baby's last breath is not a symbol.
It is a fact.

My anger is smooth, intact, decadent. I am not hungry.
I am fed, overfed, scrolling through grief I do not own,
with fingers that can afford to stop.
My stomach closes in guilt. I wish I could close
my eyes and not see, and the privilege is that I eventually do.

Some days I log off. Most days for good: as in:
I delete accounts, I refuse the language of brands,
I scrape meaning from refusal. It's not enough,
but it's what I can do while others scrape the limbs
of their brothers from trees.

This should end with fire – not metaphor.
But I only have language, and a voice
that feels both too much and not enough.

Marzia D'Amico

For Abdel

I make this bird for Abdel—
a simple, coloured paper bird.
Let it fly to him—
a message from Earth!
Let 10,000 more fly to
his brothers and sisters
who've ascended with him.

On this simple, coloured paper bird,
where nothing is enough,
I draw eyes, many eyes,
raised in seeing.
Many mouths,
open and singing.

I draw a little scene:
olive trees,
their boughs raised in greeting;
a goat, a donkey, a lizard,
running in greeting;
sky and clouds thundering
the breath of greeting.

I draw a small figure of myself,
my hands raised,
holding my heart, beating.

On this simple, coloured paper bird,
we send our simple message,
of love.

Laura Grevel

When the Weekend Comes

When the weekend comes,
we'll be munching on French fries...
but that's not a side meal
that's genocide.
Chopped up like,
children's limbs and snacking on
governments' lies,
when these Happy Meals
leave our siblings to cry.
Let's order a
Coca Cola so cool
we let its murders slide.
Make sure it's
topped up with ice
to soothe the aches of our guilt
as our pockets surrender to these
nasty consumer goods.

Or,
how about a
pumpkin spiced latte
that we share with our mates?
We want some
whipped screams
so we can suck the blood from
our straws.
I guess these
broken bones are
Finger Lickin' Good,
and these
Dunkin' Donuts powdered with soot are
the sweetest tooth to my worries.

I mean,
the world just seems too scary,
but I just don't have the capacity
to hold the world's deepest wounds
and be its greatest wonderer.
I mean, I'm not an activist
so, oh well, ceraVe!
So it's

Olay for me to
not to be okay
and take a
self-care day.
Because you're worth it.
Call me the Max Factor
but these cosmetics are worthless.
The deficit in the South
while the North sends the journalists
to mindlessly document
our failings.

Well, I just know I'm
not going to
L'Oréal because
in the floods of my tears
I cleanse my sins with Dove
at the expense of my skin.
I go to church on Sundays
to give my Lord its Soap &Glory.
We take the weight off of our
Head & Shoulders,
by talking about ourselves,
talking about our baes and
talking about our
normal days.
As if, that's normal?

Did you know Johnson's
are slipping children's stories away?
And how the world is funding colonial settlers,
while we settle in the dismissal of their truths?
What will you tell your youth,
when they ask you
if your couth is your compliance?
Not all that glitters is gold
so are you questioning Midas' touch
and what you are told by the news?
And this is not about me
telling you
what to do, for you
get to choose what
side of the story that you're on.
And, this isn't about shame,

for you will only grow better from love.
But if we are more conscious
and realise freedom is not just about
what we have in our pockets
but the ideas we invest in,
these big, capitalist giants
can feel small and powerless
when we take back the empire
that's in the making.
If Adidas can say impossible is nothing
and can get you all running then,
you are no different than a go-getter,
just a hamster on a wheel.
Don't let these big brand deals introduce
you to social justice,
when they are making the fucking crisis!

For we are
the magic in those beans.
The beanstalk grows
when we walk the talk
and if autumn can find the courage
to release the leaves
that are no longer necessary
then, so can we.
In the vision of building a
better society.
So why don't we,
take a shot at a boycott
if we can afford it?
Cause how much does it really Costa?
Justice has to be fought for
as injustice is always paid for
to ensure that what we are being sold
isn't selling our souls
in the process.
For the greatest food is wisdom.
And when these kids pick up these textbooks,
will they know that we
fought so hard for a fairer world for them?
Or will they,
Simply have to bear the burden,

once again?

So when the weekend comes,
we see that we can do something.
In fact, we can do everything,
And realise, that we're winning.

Kaia Allen-Bevan

Limbs

How can it be that hands can't feel?
Fingers never able to stroke
Or hold
Or share
That tummies can't be rubbed
Soft and smooth
Or heads scratched
Or gifts handed.

How can it be that legs can't run?
Taken, by blast. Blasphemy!
Or balls kicked
Or race won
That jumping on sand is a game for others
Soft and smooth
That I can't chase you
Or you me.

How can it be that feet can't stand?
Or pitter patter heard
Or stools climbed on
To see over the counter
& watch bread rolled
Soft and smooth
That toes can't be counted
Or tickled.

How can it be that arms can't stretch?
Sisters nudged
Brothers hugged
Blackboards can't be written on
Fruit can't be reached for
Soft and smooth
That trees can't be planted
Or climbed.

How can it be that cheeks can't press?
Your cheek against mine
My breath against yours
That I can't kiss them
Or rub them clean

Soft and smooth
Only blood runs now
Or tears.

How can it be that we can't go home?
Your bed
Rocks and rubble broke it
Blankets shredded
And flesh
Soft and smooth
Teddy gone
Or crushed.

How can it be that targets are made of you?
Habibi, my darling
A.I. and the Gospel
Drones
They know not what life is
Or what they do
The precedent of modern presidents
Or old Devils.

Amelia Harker

Arab Blood, Scottish Bones. A Scottish Palestinian mother,
observing the horror from afar.

5 Little Teeth

1 sun-dappled autumn morning, I hold your squidgy hand that fits into the centre of my ageing palm.
Your wriggly, squiggly fingers are like excited earthworms dancing to a funky tune.
This is our first day of this new adventure my little friend.
Your face tipped up to see the minute nuances of my shifting facial expressions, your eyes watching for reassurances that you are safe, we are safe.

2 people, one older, one younger walking briskly in the coolness of changing seasons. Your little backpack snuggling your shoulders, guarding your spine, cushioning your ribs.
Your eyes equally filled with love, and wonder, and excitement, and anxiety.
Your mind is trying to balance the tumultuous emotions spinning, alternating, juggling within you.
You squeeze my hand for reassurance, I squeeze it back.
I am your safe place.
I place my hand on your chin and stroke your lower jaw.

3 pops of sound come from different directions and a feeling of platonic pressure pushes our hands apart.
You are swept up into the air like an inverted roller-coaster.
I am slammed forward like a surfer on a rip tide.
There is a scream, yours or mine, or both?
Then ringing, stinging ringing that feels like my head is melting.

4 gasps of desperation to breathe, then a full breath.
Choking, coughing, blood, pain, smashed teeth.
My mind is screaming for logic, frantically searching for commandments of what to do next...
You, I remember you, I must find you.

5 seconds to remember you were thrown behind me.

5 clawing stretches to turn my body around.

5 seconds of staring into hell searching for you.

5 minutes of wading through cloth, and concrete, and shoes, and glass, and hair, and door frames, and flesh, and car headlights, and bone, and...

I have 5 little teeth that I can take, the rest of you is so small that I can't find you.

I was your safe place and I failed, I'm so sorry Bubba.
I have put your 5 little teeth in a piece of cloth tied around my neck.

Serena B. Slack-Robins

Marett Troostwyk

Gaza

Once an ice-cream truck
Now a mortuary

Gregory Woods

What's Death Got To Do With It?

We're not using sticks and stones
We're using bombs and drones
Words?
Words?
We're not using words
Table talk?
Seated?
Talks?
Let's kill some first
A few score
Or is it more?
Is it thousands
Millions?
More?
What's death got to do with it?
What's death but the final physical motion
What's death but the final physical test?
What's death but the end of second best?

We're going to protect you ....
Protect you
From God knows what
From all those
Evil forces that will bring you down
What's death got to do with it?
We couldn't give a toss
Our action is to fight economic loss
Death
Your death
Their death
No no no
Oh little ones
Oh blots on our horizon
It's economic
Stop your histrionics
It's the most precious of all
Little darlings
It's stuff
It's stuff
Like gas and oil

Like salt and fish
Like gold and diamonds
Like cobalt and lithium
Like land land land
It's not even a bluff
You're going to be stuffed
You're stuffed
Up to the gizzards
Utterly Empty
Empty inside

Frazzled Fried
Frozen
Starved
Burnt alive
Everything denied
And
That's what
That's what
That's what death's got to do with it

Claire Griffel

Remember

They say:
The world's just like this.
It's only natural that we hate,
That we divide,
That we know what's best for you.
I say: do not comply.

They say:
You must live in fear
From this group of people,
From this type of idea,
From this threat of losing everything,
So attack them before they get you.
I say: do not comply.

They say:
The truth is this, and only this,
Found in the loudest shout and bullying finger,
In the AI-fabricated image,
In the simplistic slogan you'll have seared in your mind.
I say: do not comply.

They say:
Read only this book, it'll make you believe,
Hear only this person, they'll make you believe,
See only this programme, this social media site,
It's all you need to believe.
I say: do not comply.

They say:
Justice is a prison for your freedom,
Instead, we give you what we know you want,
What we know you really feel about the others.
We give you our justice and it's good.
I say: do not comply.

They say:
Forget history.

I say:
Remember.

Jerri Daboo

Persephone's Lament, as Cavafy Hears It

A heroön stands erect,
And in it Cavafy stirs,
listening to how myths bleed,
watching—
Persephone, snatched from Spring's lush lap,
her laughter cleaved by the dark
    and lost in the deep Stygian folds.

In these lands held sacred, ancient spirits guard
   the songs of Dreamtime,
    Bunjil and Baiame sketch constellations with ancient light.

   (And Cavafy pauses to reflect on why these spiritual laws are
   not heard by the usurpers)

And Persephone, kin-stripped, is joined by the children of the
Billabong
And their mournful song is heard in Hades where the children gather
and sing
sheltering in Persephone's embrace.

    And she breathes them all in.

They come from Palestine, where young dreams lie in shattered
heaps,
And they join those spirits snatched during those junta-haunted
nights.

Cavafy's spectral voice,
Charts the stolen paths through Gaza's fiery rains,
Whispers drifting across the red dust,

   Where we swim in Stolen lands, Stolen lungs.

This threnody, this song of nations fractured,
   is again stitched into a sweaty stillness.

   Mother, the dark swallows me.

   Father, why does light flee?

Abuela, my shadow wanders.

And Persephone kneels beside the children and gently sings her lament.

> For the broken blooms of Gaza,
> For the stolen girlhoods in Argentina,
> For the child soldiers who can't remember their mother.

Cavafy's knees bend to Persephone's sweet song.
As he rests his head on the cold Earth.
He whispers to her—

> There is no journey home to Ithaka.
> No voyage returns us to the innocence we once knew.

Nicholas Manganas

Meet Me at the Plaza in Gaza

Meet me at the poolside bar, IT'S NOT TOO FAR.
At the plaza in Gaza. It's all very nice, we stayed there twice.
There's a charming lil casino. It reminds me a lot of RIO
WHERE when you ask for a shot, believe it or not.
The drink is served from a pitcher,
forged from a converted cartridge belt
it's very very chic and svelte.

The modest models there, the fashion can't compare.
Their clothing's made the motif displayed.
It's a Kevlar bikini with a flak jacket stole, it's just how they roll.
But you gotta watch out on the beach,
'cause the lifeguards compete as sharp shooters replete.
So make sure you bring your towel from the tower
'cause after an hour on the sand -
they might mistake your dark tan, for some kinda commando.
They may not understand though, you're one of the guests.
You know the rest.
Until you've confessed in the state of undress,
your testimony under duress.
And even a stress position, which we know isn't torture,
can damage the furniture and mar your stay,
on your holiday in Gaza.

It's never complete until from your seat in the theatre
where you get to hear, the children's chorus,
where they implore us for food.
And I'm told it's not rude to leave 'em to starve,
right outside in the yard.

But at the poolside cabana, not even a banana.
You gotta understand what they've done with the place. Rubble's
gone, now replaced
with a five-star café. With starving starlets galore -
they've so much fashion and more, fascist fashion galore! Hardly any,
well not much more gore.

The casino's complete,
and while there's still an occasional bombing,
let me point out INSTEAD the lovely GIVENCHY awning,
is above your head.

Time on the shooting range is still mandatory at this stage
for every looter, that you're the shooter
you can claim a stack of chips. So go 'head, let 'r rip

Richard Spisak
@rwspisak

"Ya Walladi" يا ولدي

You eventually found us, Habibi
After so many missed chances.
A quiet triumph that brought us muted joy.
We swaddled you then in Geddo's kufiya, torn from him
That morning, though miraculously unblemished.
We cradled you, and washed you when able.
Of the dust that worms into every fold, into every pore.

No matter. Cupping your ears, we softly hummed *Tahlileh Jaliliyyeh*
And others to you, savouring those moments though soured by dread.
Of the many horrors outside, including the hard metal krump
And ear-tearing violence of the bombs. The bitter, loveless abomination
Of soldiers, their fingers twitching with murderous impatience.
Or the off-whine drone of quad-copters hunting innocence from above
Profaning life and all that the poet had once dreamed of.

You came to us, Habibi
Amidst pain we had then thought unbearable.
You salved our shuttered grief with your snuffling, blurry cries
Your gurgling, cooing laugh. Though too few they seemed to us then.
Together, beneath thin scrapes of cloth that kept out neither heat, nor sound
Your soft eyes spoke of the ephemeral, of second chances and what might be.
Oh, how we cherished you Habibi. Like nothing before.

Breffní Lennon

Inspired by a tragic news story of one Gazan family who after many years of struggle, conceived a child through IVF only for their child to then die in an Israeli bombardment. "Geddo" is a term of endearment given to grandfathers in Palestine, while Tahlileh Jaliliyyeh, or "Galilean Lullaby" is a traditional Palestinian lullaby written by the poet Tawfiq Zayyad and often sung by the British Palestinian singer Reem Kelani.

Call a Spade a Spade

Generally I think we should be clear
Enough in our language, that it would be
Natural to call a spade a spade, a scythe a scythe
Or a human a human, a child a
Child, when reporting them being shot at, whilst waiting
In line for flour or clean water
Dying from starvation, as well as bombs and guns
Even now.

Hazel Warren

Shopping Trip

to the mall über alles
cometh fresh softwares
for sale as to salvage
plaster some fantastic
voyage into the sungod
and whatever duty free
can palm off on Sunday
no more crusader drone
into the hollowed land
but now bring your own
plastic bag for refuse
souls set to turn your
landfill datasets into
some memorial for each
killed in line of food
isles of chilled child
staring out of oranges
from the silence to be
marked in song contest
encrusted with diamond
or integrated circuits

Drew Milne

Beating Hearts Break Ribs

- a percussive spoken word piece

I'm tired of hiding.
My passivity wants fighting.
No more can I wait
For solutions through debate?
How long will this take?
Seems in history, it comes in waves.
We get so far
Then the far right move the bar.
The rich still gobbling caviar
The needy still living off pourboire
Agh! This friction is starting to scar.
The news feels like grimoire
I'm done leaving the door ajar
Waiting for peace and change to creep in
Whilst like toxic radiation
Fascist ideals, and policies seep in
In bed politicians and companies sleep in. Breeding.
Breathe in
I get to a point where the anger stops
Not because I'm over it
But because my cells lock
For those Caged in the cell block
Enslaved by loopholes and profit
Stop
Stand by mode pops
Fainting turns you off when there's a spanner in the cogs
Protective stagnant state
Just come back to before it's too late
Rest is rebellion but the revolution can't wait
I'm still feral with livid liberation
Desperate to Change a nation
But stuck in.....hesitation
F-f-f-frozen in indignation
I get to a point where I just don't understand
There's people who believe fellow beings should be banned?
That science isn't real
That queerness is surreal
That comfort in your skin some kind of big deal
That trans folk don't deserve safety to feel

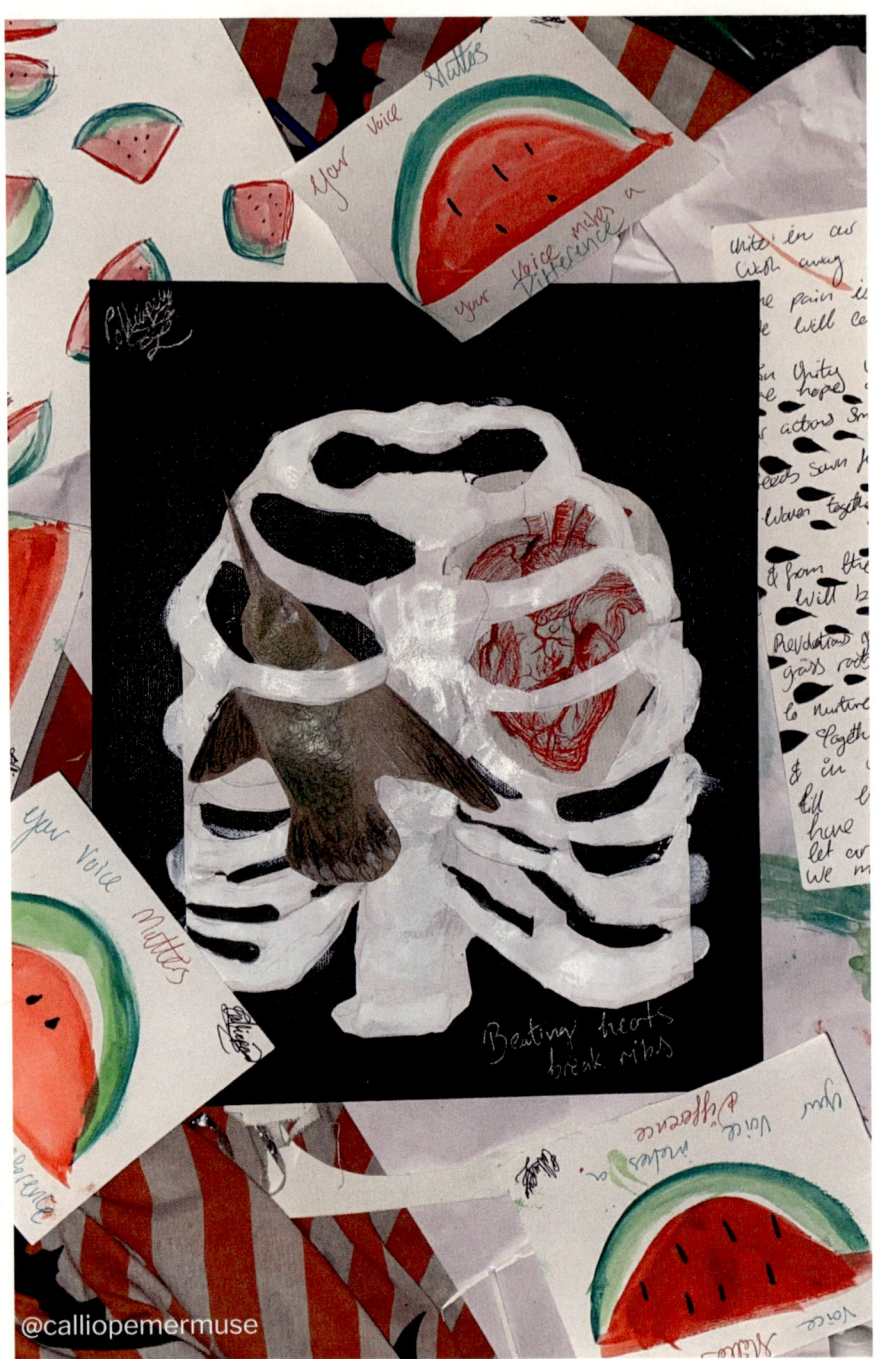

@calliopemermuse

That disabled people have no appeal
That Palestine should be occupied by Israel
That right wing ideals spun off the newsreel like thread off the
spinning wheel has facts or appeal
Pricked fingers sleep in ignorance whilst protective rose and thorn
defence is considered an offence, when we just want existence
We have data on our side of the fence
Resistance
And more importantly, love and acceptance.
The disbelief leaves me breathless and bereaved
They're angry that things change
Whilst we're mad from having to grieve
Our presence threatens their peace
Whilst our existence can't move in ease
Because their threats leave us needing frozen peas
At the very least
We just want safety for all
Yet we're considered the rebel?
I'm still angry but stuck in a confused state
Golden syrup once childhood sweet, now sticky, sickly mouldy
monarchy taste
How long will we wait
People would rather hate
Than finding ways to tolerate?
Stubborn ignorance trumps efforts to educate
Peoples would rather fight than find solutions through debate?

Oh.
Wait

Isn't that what I said?
Hmmm
We've gone full circle
Are the white supremacist cogs beginning to whirlpool
Stuck in a cycle
Some deranged loop
Soured Samsara, a Hades recital
We gotta catch it before signs get vital
We don't just need calls to action we need a cital.
I'm tired of fighting
Passivity IS hiding
My heart's hurting from beating too fast
My ribs cage the hummingbird of rage
(But at least she flies free, with you and me, together in safety)
It's our turn to act in the revolution we see

And maybe, just maybe
This time
If together we align
We can stop coexistence being a crime.

Calliope
@calliopemermuse

Unchosen

Embrace the wind
which carries the breaking voices
of anguish, at the cruel choices
that condemn.

Gather the little children
whose schools have been besieged,
shredded books in the debris.
their text drowned in vermilion.

Heal the scarred and wounded
whose targeted hospitals offer no safe refuge,
starved of resources, buckling under the deluge.
scapegoated and blood-stained.

Feed the shrunken innocents, trapped
in the engineered cull of felling famine.
Unoccupied eyes, widely bleak and barren.
The world's words, ineffective and inept.

A meaningless moment's silence,
compassion silent too long,
choked by the falsehoods spun.
Roar into existence defiance.

Hold to account the commanders
who trade death for control and power.
Sullied hands pointing at the cowered,
crying calcified crocodile tears.

N. Chamchoun

Dustfugue

Adapted from Paul Celan's Death Fugue [Todesfuge]

grey dust of night /
    you taste it in darkness
you breathe it at dawn /
    you breathe it at zenith /
        you breathe it at dusk
you drink it and drink it
you dig a grave in the sky /
    there is room

A man in the house /
    he writes /
        he plays with his shadows
he writes /
    when the light is still grey over sea
he writes /
    when your walls crumble
he whistles his dogs /
    they tear at your doors
he whistles his children to school /
    teaching them colours of dust

your golden hair Ziona /
    your ashen hair Fadwa

grey dust of morning /
    you breathe it at night
you drink it and drink it
you dig a grave in the sky /
    there is room
your child lives in the burnt house /
    your eyes are of olive /
        your voice is of wellwater
she lives under torn canvas /
    your eyes are of nightfall /
        your voice is of smoke
she lives in the camp /
    in the wind /
        in the salt
she digs a grave in the sky /
    with her hands /

with her breath

he calls it defence /
    he calls it possession /
        he calls it return
he writes Palestine /
    and means nothing remains
he writes Gaza /
    and says sand is enough for your bones

your golden hair Ziona /
    your ashen hair Fadwa
one lives in towers /
    the other wrapped in ashes and cloth

grey dust of zenith /
    you breathe it at dusk
you breathe it at night /
    death is a master from Eretz
he plays with his shadows /
    he calls the fire /
        they fall and fall /
        and fall
death is a master from the sky /
    his eye is iron
he shoots with precision /
    his house in order /
        yours in dust

a man in the house /
    your golden hair Ziona
he tears you from Land /
    only graves in the air
he plays with his shadows /
    dreaming of death

your golden hair Ziona /
your ashen hair Fadwa

Marijn Nieuwenhuis

Olive Trees

Two olive trees
on a suburban nature strip
look out of place
among the paperbarks, grey gums, bottle brush

Wattle birds hide in their branches
waiting to tackle nectar-filled grevillea nearby

A neighbour prunes the trees
collects olives in plastic tubs

I wonder about olive trees far away
tenderly cared for by hands
over generations
hands that know every leaf, bud and fruit

Trees that are bulldozed, burnt
by those who demand the land
but have no care for what grows there

We need these daily reminders
on our suburban streets –
to think about the people
who want to prune, collect olives in peace

Sarah Attfield

For Gaza, Now and Always

Doves at dawn, voices from the rubble, a luminous ray
in choreography with the dust.

Wasteland of graves, landscape of wasted dreams, repository
of dignified hope and humanity in its total absence.

For Gaza, now and always, my despair entangled with my indignation,
how can the world watch when the crows cry?

My grief is red like your blood that paints the empty streets,
my rage is flowing like your searing tears evaporating in the void
of dystopia, your land of annihilation and proud ancestry.

For Palestine, now and always, my agonistic rebellion
enmeshed with radical care and the world with their amoral delusion
stands solid in silence.

Anastasia Christou

Dark Night of the Soul

Does posting about Palestine do anything?

It's not gunna stop the genocide

So what's the point ?

Hours I stayed like this.

An ego death like never before

But one I clearly have once explored

Before.

Posting about Palestine

Has more to do with solidarity than anything else

In a world where social obedience is key to government control

Saying no

We will not obey

We will talk about Palestine

Again

And

Again.

An Act of Sorcery and Soul.

A carrier of energetic anti- compliance.

An Act that holds magnitude and depth.

An Act of Freedom.

Stop the genocide

Against our minds.

And Against the World.

Free Palestine.

Free Our Mind.

Naomi L.A 'Baudelaire' Smith

A Thoroughly Modern War

Powerful men, they crave war.
Human lives, used as bargaining chips.
I feel ashamed for my Country and of myself as I have turned
my head away.
Young soldiers, indoctrinated into shooting children in the head who
have come for food.

Human lives, used as bargaining chips.
Food and water withdrawn as the World watches on.
Young soldiers, indoctrinated into shooting children in the head who
have come for food.
Any chance of any moral victory long since gone.

Food and water withdrawn as the World watches on.
Genocide. Say it. For that is what it is. Genocide.
Any chance of any moral victory long since gone.
The haggard faces of women and wide-eyed children gaze into the
lenses of foreign TV cameras.

Genocide. Say it. For that is what it is. Genocide.
I feel ashamed for my Country and of myself, as I have turned my
head away.
The haggard faces of women and wide-eyed children gaze into the
lenses of foreign TV cameras.
Powerful men. They crave war.

Jim Lupton

Crunching Stones

Weighted by words I should have long buried
I walked my melancholy up the path
Crunching stones beneath my mind
Where hawthorn meets hornbeam
The cry for life beckons me close
Nestled within the thicket's briar
A nest bursting with broken shells
And daffodil throated blackbirds
Calling, for a chance in this game

The air no longer seemed punished
As my breath conquered the brow
Paused by a memory of last summer's dusk
When a squadron of geese from the land of the maple
Flew so low I might have touched a feather
As they fog-horned the folly of men
Who draw lines in the earth and call them countries

In the valley below
Ten acres of golden barleycorn
Ears tilting in the breeze
Listening for the harvest
As nature's balm rubs life
Into my memory
Of their death.

Daron Carey

Each different, yet part of one whole

@calliopemermuse

Command and Control

I'm struggling to work out
how many command and control centres
Hamas has?

it seems they have one in every single
tent and hospital and school
in Gaza?

there aren't many places which aren't
command and control centres -

makes you wonder what they're commanding,
it seems to mainly be children and women
who for reasons I cannot understand

cluster round these centres
not realising that the innocent Israeli Army
will accidentally bomb them

Gerald Kells

Sufficient

For Deborah C. Segal and Jennifer A. Minott - two Jewish female writers I know, and their concerns with the worldwide increase of anti-Semitism, one of the horrific end-results of what international mass media and Wikipedia have called "The Israeli-Hamas War".

The way I see it

That little symbol
Seen everywhere now
Copies a move from a chamaeleon

Doing its best
Imitation of a
Clear morning sky,

Doing its best
Imitation of still
Swimming pool water.

That little geometric shape—
Four sharp corners—
A cube the prettiest hue the sea can be

Signifies taking a stand
Against the rising tide
Wide and renewed

Against the people
Who have Semitic blood,
Against the tongue that's Hebrew—

I understand this hatred well:
The strong dislike
For *who's* different.

Our two peoples
Have endured
Slavery in the past.

Then we escaped and rebelled.
Those facts should
Make us natural allies.
Knowledge or ignorance of long-ago

Oppression encourages *some* to act
Like oppressors. Those unlike them are "lesser than".

Their hate speech the world over,
Their war moves on Gaza
Paints the bullseye on a whole people.

I am neither
Pro-Zionist nor
Pro-Israel.

Never mind state borders.
Never mind religious faith.
I am pro-you.

I knew you to be
Decent before you
Revealed your ethnicity. Therefore,

I support you.
As women.
As writers.

I will stand
At your side
When scorn comes chasing you

And defend
Your humanity in battle
As I would for any friend.

The way I see it

I don't need no blue square
To show solidarity with you.
Just my ally-ship is sufficient.

Dee Allen

The Hope of Freedom

Let freedom ring,
While Lady Liberty sings,
Let it spread like water,
Drowning the marauders,
Cleaning out the corruption,
To power up clean productions,
Melting away the violence,
In order to sprout non-violence,
Soaking up all the crazy firearms,
No more chaos to do harm,
To wither away our Constitution,
In order to think of grounded solutions,
To feed the mouths of the enslaved,
Growing seeds of support engraved,
Drifting us in another direction,
An ocean of collection and reflection.
Yes, you, please plant the tiny seed,
The seed of positivity and humanity,
Let freedom ring; hope will sprout,
Let injustice be mute; evil will drought.
Hope is inside you, her, him, and we,
Don't stop creating a liberating sea.

Edward Foreman

Communiqué

Keep up your bright swords, for the dew will rust them.
(William Shakespeare, Othello, Act 1, Scene 2)

The dew has still not rusted
the bright unsheathed swords.
There's a Golgotha in Sudan,
in Ukraine a Potter's Field,
a Gethsemane in Gaza.
Jesus says, *Enough of this!*
But pity is as deaf
as Malchus's severed ear.

Michael Durack

Winter Harvest

After violent storms
Men run, carrying slender stalks
Of girls and boys with drooping heads,
Dusty, raised in a dry land.

Hurrying them to hospital car parks
Where winnowing takes place,
Separating the living grain
From the chaff of the dead.

Rena Fleming

Bull

on each side of a fence
a bull stands in a field
taking measure they face
sensing land grab
nostrils a vent
for the geyser of indignation
building
the sudden hot fizz of a chance
pricking them
cows about them graze, heifers
belted with a shiver, the bulls
are elephants in the room

at a canter they charge
their foreheads' bulk meeting
a battering ram of bone
the wire in between
and the trampled grass
caught in the fury
beetles quick to the wing
a foray of soldier ants in smithereens
their home under the hoof
inaudible welling of weeping

Rosemary Drescher

A Boy of Gaza

2025

His mother tells him that they must be
at the Food Distribution Point
by 1am.
The bag of flour will dim the hunger pangs
for one more day.
The gathering point is a 'Turkey Shoot'
for Israeli Army snipers.
A good opportunity to get some practice in.

A shot cracks out. His mother falls.
In panic, his little brother runs, anywhere,
clutching one of her blue shoes.

Later, at the bombed out hospital, he and his father
look for them.
He has a battered backpack.
It's used to carry food, he says.

Opening it, he takes out a cloth garment.
His father has the same in his.
'It's our burial shrouds', he says.

A boy of Gaza.

Israel, you have sown for yourself - Dragon's Teeth.

Cathal Mac Thréinfhir

Gaza, Palestine

Cities rushing
dissonate their rhythms.

Streets discussing
fall silent.

Squares gathering
are emptied.

Markets haggling
shutter their stalls.

Minarets summoning
cease their calls.

Schools teaching
close their doors.

Hospitals treating
clear corridors.

Roads clogging
now lead only away.

Duck
Run
Hide
Cover
Run

Through the dust,
	prayers rising,

		like lifted stones,
		rebuilding home.

Charles Josefson

A Picture from Gaza

The bone-colored buildings gleam,
reflecting the heat of the high sun,
recalling a younger, peaceful time.
First glances are deceptive;
closer looks show something missing.
Here and there, a window pane shines,
but almost all the glass is gone now,
all the window frames shattered.
Tattered curtains hang like flags,
shifting little in the fitful breeze.

Inside the apartment, shadow rules.
Having nowhere to go, broken walls
and blocks of ceiling are now a floor.
Dust covers everything, waits silent
for further bombardments to lift it.
Only the man sitting on the bed,
suit worn but clean, shoes polished,
is exempt from the dust, any shadow.
He and the wind-up Victrola, black vinyl
spinning the Pastoral through pipe smoke.

Lennart Lundh

Sadly, this poem was originally written in 2018 as "A Picture from Aleppo." I'm a Vietnam veteran (discharged as a conscientious objector), and my oldest grandson is a veteran of America's stupidity in Afghanistan (discharged due to PTSD that still haunts him fifteen years later). We never seem to learn, do we?

No Bloody Gauze in Gaza

No hell below us ... John Lennon

Imagine a child too young to know of dreams
or what a nightmare is: a baby that can't tell you
what is wrong and yet knows that something is.
Imagine you can see her with your own eyes,
feel it all sit like a clot in your aching heart.
Imagine witnessing a doctor ration the last roll
of precious gauze in Gaza, the gaze of a camera
showing you a beautiful Madonna and Child
scene until it pans-out – further – to give you
the much bigger picture – the confused infant
and the fraught mother crying in untempered pain.
Imagine no morphine there, to numb the ends
of the little half-legs remaining – the lower halves
still caught, lost in dry rubble or under the cloak
of a snare of words in the glare of a gaslit mantle.
Imagine a panning-out further, then a zooming-in
on a tear-filled eye or on a powerless incubator.
Imagine no relief in this strip of razed land bereft
of clean water, electricity, basic medical supplies.
Imagine a barbaric jugging: the shape-shifting
nature of a bawling baby or a hare-like creature
or other animals being stewed in a bloody bubble.

John D Kelly

In My Office

I am sitting in my office.

I am sitting in my office I hear the sound of the air conditioner

I am sitting in my office I hear the sound of the air conditioner
I eat my lunch

I am sitting in my office I hear the sound of the air conditioner I eat
my lunch I open my social media of long-term choice and through the
empires of images I find myself facing Marwan Makhoul's poem on
the bombs and the birds I find myself facing words I find myself facing
words under words I find myself facing words I find myself facing a
comment that calls the love for songbirds an invitation to terrorism

                                                    I know the drill

Dismembered bodies must be
Silenced to grab
Land The bird of Palestine
Is the sunbird
The birds of Palestine are
Sparrows and hawks
And geese and eagles and swans
I know this I
Don't know much more I can't picture

The world to hold its breath when hell comes down to hearth
What was the exact moment
When the fragrance
Of olive wood the silence
By the old wall
Of Jerusalem became
Absurdity
          Mohamoud?
Raafat's kite, with my eyes closed I hope

To feel you above my head
Sliding across
A sunshine without terror

Things have their plasticity Things go back to their plasticity when I open my eyes Things are determined by their distance and their capacity to change and their capacity to impact on each other Things are determined by their capacity to be pulled apart Things are determined by their capacity to come together The only thing I can do is to think of blockages and protests and workers enacting blockages The only thing I can think of is the act that is difficult to do The refusal of sending weapons the refusal of shipping goods to Israel The refusal of silence Refusal of not protesting Things go back to their plasticity I hear the sound of the air conditioner I am sitting in my office

Things have their plasticity Things go back to their plasticity when I open my eyes Things are determined by their distance and their capacity to change and their capacity to impact on each other Things are determined by their capacity to be pulled apart Things are determined by their capacity to come together The only thing I can think of is that my break is almost over I hear the sound of the air conditioner I am sitting in my office

The only thing I can think of is that my break is almost over I hear the sound of the air conditioner I am sitting in my office

I hear the sound of the air conditioner I am sitting in my office

I am sitting in my office.

Fran Sani

Where I Begin

We are mosaics — pieces of light, love, history, stars.

— *Anita Krizzan*

I am the scent of rain on bounded ground,
where stories rise like steam from moss and root.
Each syllable from my mother's tongue tastes like home —
soured fruit, sweetened tea,
the ghost of a lullaby,
only half-remembered.

I was born head-first,
into the thick of it —
a world already mid-sentence.
I glide and punch,
as if time itself couldn't decide
whether to hurry or hold.

Air tickles my skin,
like a mother parting hair with weathered fingers.
I hear power in the whisper of an unused canvas,
words flying like bunting,
before landing softly
inside the depth of a grieving chest.
My eyes drink colour:
the bruise-blue of evenings,
sunflowers stitched into the spine of a neighbouring hill,
a flicker of peace
held steady like prayer.

Water knows my name,
flowing through muscle,
humming beneath ribs.
It carries the salt of grief and bloodline,
everything I've lost,
everything that waited —
patient as tide.
Fire lives in my heels —
a strong beat, a sudden turn.

It's the sharp snap of dance
on cracked concrete,
the forge of a voice
rising from silence.

The moment I said no,
and the world heard it.

Spirit is the fifth element,
not touch,
but being touched —
by something vast and unseen.
A hush in the crowd
when a word finds its mark.
Free flow. Bound awe.

And when the party starts —
Earth arrives first.
Shoes muddy, hands full,
bringing food no one asked for,
but everyone eats.
She nods once,
then finds a corner to listen.
She stays after the music ends,
sweeping petals into her pockets.

Air follows,
drifting sideways through a window
that wasn't open.
She doesn't speak —
just flutters and folds,
a poem caught in the hem of her sleeve.
Your hair ends up braided
with someone else's story.

Water slips through the back door,
smelling of salt and rain.
She hugs you too long.
You cry, and don't know why.
She doesn't dance —
she moves like memory.

At some point, you realise
it's her heartbeat
the whole room is moving to.

Fire kicks the door in laughing.
She starts the music over.
She makes people dance

who swore they never would.
You argue with her at midnight,
forgive her at two.
She leaves sparks on your sleeve.

Spirit was already there.
Lit the candles. Tuned the speakers.
You don't see them —
but when the right word lands,
the hush feels holy.
They nod from the doorway
just as dawn breaks.

So here, among pages and petals,
beneath the bright weight of history,
I gather myself —
from the five senses,
from earth, air, fire, water —
and the one that lives
between breath and movement.

I begin — again —
with every story
that remembers me back.

Abigail Hutchison

Twin Tragedies in Gaza

Hold a Mirror to Our Humanity

Ten years and three IVF rounds, Naeim
and Wissam of five months lost in seconds
in Rafah. Come summer massacre,
Asser and Aysell bombed in supposed safety,
births registered just as devastation
stole their fragile lives. Winter brings hypothermic
deaths - Jumaa in a bleak, frozen tent,
lonely the day after twin Ali froze
in cold of Gaza Martyrs' hospital.
Saba and Sana sleeping, woke screaming
in Tuffah neighbourhood, dying at four.
Sally and Dalia's lives cut short, bombed,
before they could pursue their dreams
studying engineering in Ontario.
Shocked silence deafening as even scarce
freedom lost in multiple double grief.
And these a fraction of the children lost.

Gaza Twins Asser and Aysell

My wife was tired, four days after the birth
by Caesarean section, of our twins,
miracle boy and girl to celebrate.
But tragedy struck, as has already
to one hundred and fifteen newborn babies,
latest safe home bombed, mothers taken,
in shroud with Asser and Aysell, names registered
just as bombs ignored their being,
and stole their fragile lives.
Injustice cries the world in vain,
but stories are now being told
by witnesses who cannot be denied
their truth of massacre or genocide.
I kneel beside. There must be peace for all.

Jane Flint Bridgewater

Jane Wignall

@

I scroll through images
of my daughter dying
or at least close to death.

Clothed in layers of concrete dust
from the targeted bombing
of her civilian apartment block.

My mum is already dead, presumed,
under rubble. My father is nowhere
to be seen and hasn't been for the last

days. My beautiful sister Bisan
@wizard_bisan1 keeps me up
to date when she is still alive

and can find clean water,
electricity and powerful falafel.
Bread made from building materials.

They can't get the miscarried blood
out of the abluted hospital sheets
so I have a look at my Stories

finish my sandwich, think about
clicking Send on a donation to the IRC
that came up on my feed but I'll do it

later. I've only got 5 minutes
of my break left. So I clean my space,
switch off my notifications.
Put my phone on silent.

Catherine Marina

Grief Café for Gaza

We hold vigil, online, and give ourselves
to a space we can't define:

Can I feel this? Can I allow myself to feel
this? I think to myself, before realising I
am already wiping away tears. I realise
that I

will survive the feeling of this. After all,
the feeling is heavy, but it is not rubble.

The rage tears you up, but it is not a
bomb.

The release empties you out, but this is
no famine — people speak, so many

voices and words — all different ways to
say sorry —

I wanna break something. I wanna break
my hands. I don't want Palestinians to be
ethnically cleansed. I think about the
sacredness of life. I am angry. I am a
mother. I am a shaman. I am ashamed. I
am Palestinian. Remember our humanity.

We are together in our loneliness. I know
no-one here but we are one. All saying
Free Palestine with our hands.
With our hearts.

Afterwards, I log off and sit. I just sit.
There are no tears.
I have to make dinner.
Tonight, I learnt about the four men
bombed for just walking in Khan Younis.
I have to make dinner.

Lahraeb Munir

Café

today I sit in a garden for the dead

where flowers bloom
and water trickles as the
dying drink tea.

I have coffee
and a teacake with butter
and strawberry jam.

the teacake is over toasted
and the coffee
too weak

but it seems churlish
to complain
to the soon to be dead

so I eat and drink
and enjoy the flowers
and sunshine. watch those

soon to die, sit in the warm, summer
air and listen to bees as they buzz
around daisies, roses and lavender.

I eat my over-toasted teacake and
weak coffee and think, this could be
someone's last food and drink.

this is someone's
last food and drink.

Ian Chapman

Utopia

I

I have found a vein.

Keeping it open means
a reading on Zoom,
where no travel or small talk
is heaven to me.

I don't have to see anyone
or be seen. I can plead
technical difficulties,
like the fifth,

listen partially,
scratch around for ideas,
snatch shiny phrases
like a magpie with a notebook.

I can eye other living rooms,
look through each window
into every life.

II

Tonight's open mic.

Ron reads first. Always funny,
he writes to read, and
the alloy of his voice and speed
galvanise his subject,
this a riff on Trump's riviera
everyone embraces as a break
from the news painting
the apocalypse.

Ron doubles down on Trump's idiocy
with a resort thronged by tourists
peppered by gunfire. He finishes,
to joyous encouragement, apologetic,
because he made his point

without picking a side.

Next, a man whose name I miss
reads and reads and reads
a Holocaust piece
which is harrowingly brilliant,
if overlong, from what I glean,
as I'm consumed by its choosing.

I think he's trying to say
'All of this happened to us.'

But no one has forgotten
so he finishes to silence.
Only the MC offers kindness
and I'm so uncomfortable and wary
of seeming an anti-Semite
that I click the applause icon,
as I will for the rest of the night,
while I marvel at the absurdity
of the world I live in.

We roll on quickly,
but I'm paralysed,
until a woman
detonates our evening.

She reads
image after image

of wounded, starving,
dead children
piled high
asking
how Gaza isn't
a gas chamber
And I just sit
in my apartment's
comfortable dark
choosing to be myself,
not everyone else,
watching the sun
burn out.

William Patrick

We Will Not Die in Silence

I won't tell you of her torn limbs—
But of her dreams.
Of laughter once filling a house,
A house that once stood whole.

Today, I won't speak of the darkened truth,
Of a holocaust committed in complicit silence,
That swallows children by the hundreds,
Crushing elders' bones,
Scarring women and men alike.

While you awaken from gentle sleep,
They do not stir from their eternal one.
They vanish by night—
While you rest your weary limbs,
The killing machine snatches them soundlessly.
No screams. No noise.

As you sip your morning coffee,
The living among them rise
To face another battle—
To survive another day,
Or to be erased.

You drop your children at school.
They search with theirs for scraps to burn,
To cook a meal,
To carry water.

No one crowds your bathroom doors,
But they must queue for hours.

Have you heard of camps of detention?
Of tents where death hovers,
Where its voice screams day and night?
Have you heard of birds that bring death?
Of drones that buzz like locusts?
Death-tech has advanced—
You'll see things in Gaza
You'll find nowhere else.

It may disgust or astound you—
That artificial intelligence
Has been summoned to kill
As many children as possible.

Yes, don't be shocked.
Killing squirrels or sparrows is forbidden—
But killing tens of thousands of children
Over years? Allowed.

The war has not ended.
And we don't know where it will.
Will genocide succeed
And leave none behind?
Or will humanity awaken
And shackle the rabid beast?

live in the age of "possible"—
Of international law,
Of human rights,
That apply only to some.

An age where neglecting a child's lunch
Is a crime,
But denying water and medicine
To thousands behind a wall

Is policy.
I wanted to tell you of Salma,
Who fled her lovely home—
Her room, her toys—
To live in a school.
She once loved her school,
But never wished to sleep on its hard floor
Or wake to bombs
Burning her neighbors.
Now Salma hates school,
And every school in the world
That failed to teach humanity
Its ABCs.

Yet Salma is luckier than Nada.
That friend fled with her family
To a tent in the south.

One night,
After fear and the falling bombs,
She closed her eyes—
And never opened them.

The tent burned with her inside.
None of them woke again.

The world saw
A scorched wheelchair—
Her brother's—
But the world did not stir.
Nor did the sleepers
On the other side of the wall.

Did I say wall?
Yes.

In 2025, there are still walls.
High concrete barriers,
Ruled by cutting-edge tech.
No one enters.
No one leaves.

Even the birds
Burn if they approach.
It is not a state, dear sirs—
But dozens of kilometers
Of siege, starvation,
Nightly explosions.

I cannot tell you the number
In that death camp—
It drops by the day.

Does it remind you of something?
Of something you read
In your history books?

I'll leave you to search.

And from my friends in Gaza,
The message is this:

**If we must die—
We will not die in silence.**

Reem Farajallah

Imagine

Death stretches up, clicks his back into shape
Wipes his skeletal brow beneath his jet-black hood
And rattles a smile in his fleshless jaws

Enough is enough that's what he'd say
Too much work for me today
I've tolerated too much of your murderous ways
There's too much blood in this slaughterhouse world
Too much pain even for me
And I'm the master of tragedy

And each of his vertebrae click into line
He stretches his toes and begins to climb
Over the rubble of a family home
And releases nine souls into dust filled air

Above in the sky a mechanical drone
Tilts a bit, turns and flies away
Death looks on with invisible eyes
And follows it back to its steel-clad dome.

A soldier high-fives his youthful mate
And in so doing seals his fate
The soldier looks where Death's eyes should be
There are bodies and limbs and a screaming face

Have you come for me the soldier says
I don't want to die
Much worse than that comes Death's reply

Death turns his back and away he strides
The soldier falls to his knees, surprised.
In the soldier's head the image grows
Spreads out of his brain and down to his toes

It wasn't my fault
They made me do it.

And Death looks back
They always say it.

Deb Michel

Gaza

From a bird's eye view
charred and scorched
like bits of charcoal
scattered across
the land after fire.

In between settlement blocs
Commanders and leaders
fight for borders
conflict and displaced refugees
see terror in occupation
war crimes in the making.

Desperation in eyes
there's nothing left here
no food either
and the war is far from over
a flood of aid is needed
for the people of Gaza.

Contemplating peace – I meditate on prayer
for an end to violence, oppression and uncertainty.
A focus on food, water, medicine
and other humane aid.

Will Isreal ever make the desert bloom?
in 'A land without people for a people
without a land'.

Or is it The Promised Land?
Light can always enter shade
but for how long can historical origins remain.
And how many hostages can ever be retained?
Boundaries for Democracy
Ceasefire Now!

John P Hindle

Forget-me-not

I think of peace, like spring.
Like sapling trees in mudreplete ground,
or primrose necks,
bending at the weight of a world at war.
The slenderness of such stalks eluding the strength
residing in the rootwebs underneath.
Is that true for us too?

I breathe peace, like pollen.
Knowing it not as disease, but more
as the unease with which we cease to appease
the lulling chills of winter.
Just like that of war.

Pollen polluting that which is dead with what is alive,
surely this is true, for us too?
Tulip buds scratching at our memories,
so entrenched in winter's sickness.
Those of light before the dark, remember?
Darkness first a cover then the captor,
anti-war wishes, like willow branches
caught in the denseness of December.

But willows spring to life in February,
did you know?
Catkins calling for their comatose sun,
like the springing awake of a dormant truce.
Willows weeping is the sign of seasons grieving,
those we lost to winter's will.
But grief can be deceiving,
can you not tell?
Tears first sting the cheek, then flush away the pain.
Salty and stark is the breeze of renewal,
no power, no fervour, like that of spring rains.

And so, I think of spring like peace.
As did the Ancient Greek - or so I've been told.
The seasonal embodiment of Eirene,
Eirene herself, the personification of peace
and the gatekeeper of eiar, all in one.

Her cornucopia awash with crocus,
her sceptre shining bright by snowdrop shroud,
her rhyton replete with hyacinth and hellebore.
Her words born from and borne by
those pollen winds:
Forget-me-not, Forget-me-not, Forget-me-not

Nico Edwards

Marett Troostwyk

Gaza

A child's back, close-buttoned
juts of bones.
From nape to hip
corseted in starvation.

Those chosen
to die
random as love
almost,
but for history
        endlessly
repeating.

Where does the savagery start?
Whisper, nudge, shove
club, rob, shave,
starve, shoot, gas -
in an orderly fashion.
And all our yesterdays
creep back to hate
and the cloven clutch
of the conmen
cranches the heart of justice.

Always, there are the studies
to make all perfectly rational;
brains mapped like territories
high value, supine, not worth
talking about.
The trickery and the jackboot;
we are not conquering you
we are liberating you.
The more intelligent,
like us, will agree.

This month, for example,
some are examining
entry wounds
focused, allegedly, in sequence
on crania, abdomen, testicles.
For rougher tastes
there is on offer
plenty of dirty feet
stampeding the ashed earth.
And veils flying
like wintered flags
as they are made to kill
each other.

To live.

The best can be done
is to collar flour;
a plump cargo
that will likely spill
between the shots.
Blood, guts splutter
for all they are worth
into the stour.

Out of which rises
a new Jerusalem,
of glistering towers;
the first resort
of the good old boys
intent upon
the wildest
badass sprees
east of Eden,
a fabulous investment.

And here we are
in Kent and Christendom
assuming
none of this ever had
the slightest thing
to do with us.

Look

we got you,

again.

We got our cold eye

on life, on death.

and you gonna

do

what?

Tess Hurson

Christmas is Coming

Christmas is coming

& Netanyahu,
like Herod,
slaughters Palestine's children.

Wise men & women pay homage
to the child in the rubble.

But their tribute
does not come with the ring
that will bind the demon
of genocide.

Ambrose Musiyiwa

The Butterfly Who Stayed in Gaza

They were accusing me of planning to leave,
as if my small wings could turn away from this land.
As if I could abandon my own in famine and fire,
and survive without the collective strength of my people.

Yes, the world has turned its eyes away.
Their voicelessness is louder than the bombs,
their amnesia is sharper than the hunger.
But we -
we will not abandon each other.
We will not forget the names of our dead,
nor let the occupiers steal our resilience and laughter.

Do not mistake that I am abandoning this land.
I am not the world.
I am not their blindness.
I am the embodied spirit of this pious land,
I am your brother, sister, son and daughter,
I am your shadow in these broken and colonised streets.

Each morning, we open our eyes,
and stand together, we win.
Each night, we hold our hands,
and endure the bombings; we fight.
The world may have escaped,
but with our stubbornness, we survive.

We are the *Butterfly of Gaza*
and though the sky falls each night,
we rise with hope each morning.
Neither have we escaped Gaza,
nor Gaza has abandoned us.
The world may have forgotten Gaza,
but Gaza has not forgotten itself.

We together fight with wounds
and unbroken flame.
We together fight under one breath
with enduring pain.
We fight for freedom, dignity, and our land.

We are the butterflies of Gaza
and though we may be small, fragile, and hunted,
our spirit will not break.
Neither can the oceans drown our names,
nor can the settlers bind us with chains.
We are the butterflies of Gaza,
and our spirit will not break.

Satkirti Sinha

Tea?

I watch as the cup is placed carefully in the saucer
The handle turned to my right
Placed carefully in front of me

The pot lifted high so the liquid flows cleanly into the cup
Just the right amount
Stopped with a flourish of the wrist

The air in the fall giving it that indefinable quality
A moment of peace
A taste of home
A memory of
Before

Lytisha Tunbridge

Freckle

I noticed a tiny freckle on your soft white hand today.
You lay next to me, on the cosy bed.
Tired from Minecrafting.
Playing superheroes.
Eating ice cream.

I hadn't noticed it before.
The freckle.
Just a tiny fleck of brown.
A dot.

Just like you.
A little dot.

I thought it might be chocolate.
Licking my finger,
Trying to get it off.

But it stayed.
Perfectly, imperfect.

It stayed
Exactly where it's supposed to be,
Your little hand in mine.

I thought of other mothers,
Searching for their children.
Amongst the rubble.
Looking for a little hand.
Searching for that familiar freckle.
                    Searching.

Sarah Attwell

Milk Turns Heavy

I hold my son the way a coastline holds the sea—
arms curved,
the shape of protection
I wish could stretch across maps.

On the news,
a mother gathers her child
the way you gather broken glass—
careful, trembling,
knowing some pieces will cut you forever.

In Gaza,
a mother is whispering names
over rubble,
over smoke,
over a body that was once the whole sky to her.

I count his breaths,
his lashes,
the soft rise of his chest—
as if counting could stop bombs,
as if naming could rebuild homes.

The milk I fed him this morning
turns heavy in my chest—
a river dammed in grief,
because there are children
whose hunger will never end,
whose cries will never be answered
in their mother's language.

I rock him,
and the earth rocks too—
but somewhere else it shakes for other reasons.

I am a mother.
She is a mother.

And the distance between us

is nothing more than seconds—
her loss,
my fear.

Alexandra Jorg

Gaza: Grief is Not Defeat

in dedication to my late sister and activist Kesra Shakir

Gaza Gaza don't you cry
We will never let you die
We may be far, we may not hear
But in our hearts we hold you dear
Every day our tears are falling
You may not see but we are mourning
All the children who have been slain
This massacre not in our name
Oh Gaza Gaza, we stand with you
We see your pain, we know it's true
Leaders of the world dismiss
The death of children goes amiss
Where has gone humanity?
This genocide is plain to see
How do leaders sleep at night
Whilst Gaza is a death site
Families dead and children killed
Hundreds daily blood is spilled
When will end these crimes of war ?
Until the people are never more?
Oh Gaza Gaza our hearts have broken
But the world has now awoken
Unity and all as one
It is now, the time has come
So let's speak out and use our voice
This has to end there is no choice
Oh Gaza Gaza don't you cry
We will never let you die.

Syra Shakir

How to Stand Aside

The leaves stayed longer on the trees that year and when the wind came it drowned out the sound of cars from the top road as I made a list of places I would never visit starting with Sudan standing in the Market Square I listened to women recite the names of the children who had died in Palestine which is when I watched people walking past meeting their families for Sunday lunch shopping for slippers and someone invited me for a coffee after my mother died the family flew in from Ireland and we had sandwiches and cake in a room near a chapel not far from the sea which is what I thought of when I heard that a child from northern Iraq had died in a boat off the coast on the bus home I read a poem out loud to my friend who told me that women in Afghanistan are not allowed to speak in public as we passed the hospital where a tree had been dragged up by its roots the earth loosened in the rain and I imagined a woman of my age sitting on the ground rubbing her feet hardened her hands hardened in a country hotter than here colder than here. 'Poetry makes nothing happen' I said, and no one stopped me.

Cathy Symes

A Ghazal for Reem and Khaled

With a kiss on your cheek, your dangling hand, you've awoken the world,
Too young for a war or to fight for your land, you've awoken the world.

By an accident of birth on one side of a barricade that seems
So ancient beside the three years your life spanned, you've awoken the world.

Through the power of love and horror now scarred into a billion hearts
As your Grandfather's tears scarred lifeless sand, you've awoken the world.

In every taste of a sweet tangerine, we will keep play in our hearts
As we go out across the Earth to demand, you've awoken the world.

We may only know you as the limp, grey body of a small child
But we remember all you were beforehand, you've awoken the world.

Photographs of a little girl with the sweetest smile, sparkling eyes,
Who, like us all, learned to talk, to crawl, to stand, you've awoken the world.

These words should never have been written, no artworks made, videos shared,
Your funeral never so suddenly planned, you've awoken the world.

You were loved so much, treasured, tried to keep safe, you just wanted to play,
I wish I never knew you or Khaled Nabhan - you've awoken the world.

Collateral

The manes of the people of the dusts bristle and burn
as they murmurate above the furies whipped
up by their neighbours' frenzied gambles.

The people of the dusts swirl around bulldozed debris
plucking the plastic from its crevices that hunger
teaches them might be bartered for Koshari.

The people of the dusts live with faltering hope that all
their neighbours' due debts will be called in before
the last of them become shrouded by the dusts.

Meanwhile,
oblivious to the eddies of the people of the dusts,
the neighbours and their friends' motorcades
speed on.

Trevor Wright

Awakening

It is the moment of awakening
I see a light turned on,
I submit to the purpose, of climbing out of my swamp.

The soul connection is so strong like a magnetic pull
to find my way home.

So the journey begins with high hopes,
my form of love can change the world.

I see possibilities in different ways of perception,
I want to build communication, to open gates of growth and yield to
destiny's flow.

I am feeling the ability to break these social walls
that are standing between us and preventing our goals
but my love and light is taken for granted.
I've been fed with half-effort and lies
this loving and hating dynamic makes it impossible for the bigger
picture to appear.

I knock back my self-worth, excuse the negativity
but the only thing my heart is really craving,
is peace, stability and clarity
raw authenticity.

Standing today in my truth
I can tell the only way forward is to let go control and surrender
to the purpose of my own soul.

Magdalena Szczerba

The King and the Moon

A huge orange moon cast its eerie glow over the battered and broken landscape. Rusty steel bars poked out of concrete boulders and hidden amongst the tortured landscape was a roofless school building. Inside it, schoolchildren lay on the floor, their emaciated bodies like chicks fallen from a nest, ribs covered only with a thin veneer of pale skin, eyes bulging with hope and fear.

The teacher passed around a small bowl of soup and a bottle of water. "Ok children, its bed time. Try and sleep and don't worry about the noise of the jets overhead or the shell fire in the distance."

"Can we have a story miss?" Begged the children.
"We need rest," replied the teacher "now, come on, sleep."
"I can't sleep miss, not with the man in the moon staring down at us."

"The man in the moon?"
"Yes miss, look."
One of the children pointed up to the night sky and sure enough there he was, a great big orange face staring down at them.
"How did he get there, miss?"
"If I tell you will you promise you'll go to sleep?"
The children nodded.

"Once upon a time many years ago in a distant land there lived a cruel and greedy King. He sat on a huge throne. It was carved out of the darkest ebony from the Brazilian rainforests. His crown was forged from the purest gold mined in the far reaches of the Gobi Desert and it was encrusted with huge sparkling diamonds from the southern tip of Africa.

Everybody in the palace bowed down to him whenever he was in sight. Anyone who forgot to bow would be taken to the castle dungeon never to be seen again.

The King relished his power over others. People competed with each other to please him. Lavish gifts would be presented to him. He was given lions and elephants, Arab stallions and peregrine falcons, Roman chariots and bronze statues, Aztec gold and Indian silks. His every desire was catered for.

In the village outside the castle walls, the people lived in humble wooden shacks and made ends meet by living off the land. Each week the King would send his tax men to take what little they had left after they had eaten.

With the taxes, he paid his army of warriors to plunder the world's greatest treasures. He ordered his men to do anything it took in order to get him riches. His warriors always returned with rare and beautiful things. One day the King ordered four of his strongest warriors to find him the most valuable objects on earth.

The first one returned with a huge uncut diamond.
'Master, this beautiful stone was unearthed deep below the ground in a remote part of Russia.'
'Never mind where it was found,' snarled the King. 'How much is it worth?'
'It is worth millions, sire,' answered the warrior.
The second warrior returned with a huge nugget of gold.
'Your Majesty. This nugget was mined beneath the fertile soil of Mexico.'
'I don't need a geography lesson!' shouted the King. 'How much is it worth?'
'It is worth millions, sire,' said the warrior.

The third one returned with a huge marble statue of a Greek god. 'Your majesty, this statue was pulled out of the crystal clear waters of the Mediterranean Sea. It is said to have once stood in the lost city of Atlantis.'
The King scanned the statue with lustful eyes. 'How much is it worth?'
'It is worth millions, sire,' replied the warrior.

The fourth warrior returned empty handed. The King flew into a rage. 'Where is my treasure?' he yelled.
'I have no treasure for you, your majesty. I have brought a wise man from the Middle East. The villagers say that he knows the whereabouts of the greatest treasure and that only he can take you there'.

The wise man stood there. His hair was long and straggly, his robe was tattered and dusty and his bare feet looked sore and gnarled as if he had never owned a pair of shoes. The King screamed at the warrior and asked him how he dared present him with a common peasant.

He turned to the wise man, 'How dare you come to me, the greatest, most powerful, most successful King in history without wearing a suit'.

The King paced up and down stamping his feet. With each step his heart pounded faster, his eyes became darker and his brow grew damp with sweat. His orange face became blood red. A great greed came over him. He wanted more. 'I want the greatest, treasure in the whole world and I want it now!' he roared, before collapsing in a heap.

As he lay on the floor the wise man walked over to him. He held out a hand to the King.

'Why should I take your hand'? whispered the King.
'I am here to show you the greatest treasure there is,' replied the wise man.

The King held on to the man's hand. He felt his heart racing. The feeling was so overwhelming and powerful and magical that he looked into the eyes of the man and smiled. The King and the man began to rise up into the sky, they climbed higher and higher. The higher they climbed the more relaxed and gentle the King became until eventually they landed on the soft powdery surface of the moon.

'So where is the treasure?' asked the King

The wise man gently lifted his hand and pointed to a huge blue circle floating in space.

'Why it is the most amazing treasure I have ever seen,' said the King, rubbing his hands together.
'Is it for me?' said the King 'What treasures can be found in the circle?'
'Oh, there are diamonds and gold, King. However, they won't make you happy. For what you are looking at is planet earth. The greatest treasure is fresh water and clean air.'

The King laughed and the wise man disappeared. Five days later he returned to find the King staring at the earth.
'I need water,' pleaded the King. 'I will give you the world's largest diamond in return for one glass of water,' he begged.
The wise man gently shook his head.

'I will give you a thousand bars of gold for a lungful of clean air,' said the King.

Again, the wise man shook his head. The King looked at the man.

'Who are you, what do you want with me?' asked the King.

'I am love, I am empathy, I am kindness,' replied the man. 'You had the power to create peace and love on the earth yet you chose greed, death and destruction. Look down on the earth, King. Look down and light up the night sky. Spread light on the greatest treasure.'

With that the man rose higher and higher until the King turned to dust. If you look up at the moon you can still see his orange face looking down, shedding light in the darkest places."

Andy Winters

Child of God

Where are you going O child of God?
I go to my school and why do you ask?
And what will you do there O child of God?
I will do my rule and be put to task.

And what is that noise O child of God?
It's the numbers in my head and why do you say?
And what is that light O child of God?
It's the shine in my eyes when I do pray.

And what is that tear O child of God?
Because I know who you are and I must away
Then come with me do not be afraid
Your garden awaits please do not delay.

And what is that smile O child of God?
Because I know who I am what more can I say?
And who is that O child of God?
The light of the world now let us away.

Bill Pook

I wanted to support the children of Gaza. The inspiration for the poem came from a French carol " L`Enfant de Dieu." The words I have written to go with the tune describe an angel challenging a child before the angel takes the child to heaven.

@calliopemermuse

Remembrance Day

the poppy I wear
blooms inside my chest
a red heart amongst the thistle.

lest we forget
before the lapel pins
there was this :

the body of a boy
face-down in Flanders mud
his bullet-hole blood red as poppies.

weeds burrow through
tuber roots deep beneath the tombstones
fallen fighting over half an inch of soil.

affix your poppy to a Union Flag,
wrap yourself up in patriotism.
by battle standards I sit in silence,

count all the goddamn bullets
buried in that boy's back,
fingering uncountried mud.

my poppy tears like a paper heart
planted in my battlefield chest.
'why aren't you wearing one?'

lest we forget.

Teo Eve

Blind Eye

The first time I saw a real dead body, uncensored
was a little boy face down on a grey beach
he could have been asleep
but for the thin sheen of water
lapping at his cheeks
carried to the shore to be recovered
from shoals of sand
as if he hadn't been alive the day before
as if his mouth hadn't watered at the smell of food
when he had his final meal
before his family took their leave
as if he hadn't giggled on his parent's knee
as they tried to distract him from the perils at sea
as if he hadn't cried in the face of the unknown
stepping into the boat
and for the home left behind
as they were forced to retreat
his name was Ahmed
his family had fled for a better life
that felt within reach
ventured into tenebrous seas
to face more hardship and hostility
chasing a desperate, hopeful dream

I've seen more dead children and babies since
missing the back of their skulls, limbs torn apart
burns etched on every inch of their skin
watched the death rattle as they took their last breath
and each time wondered the last thought
behind their eyes
prayed they were unaware and felt full
of the love in their lives
imagined the grief tearing parents apart
at the thought of never again hearing their child laugh
at facing the rest of their eternity here on this earth
without the sweet soul that between them
they birthed

I see the world turn away at each tragedy
ignoring the pain caused by their cruel apathy
and I wonder, is it the brown skin

or because to face their part in it is inconvenient?
cuz it feels like it's both
mixed with the lies of the media
and just a touch of subservience

Jess Gibson

Canticle of the Warhead

Clouds shackled, noisy with engines.
Fallen streets remember
the riverbeds of Eden.

The earth said:
All power is borrowed.
All flesh is fuel.

The child runs, carrying bread—
he does not know he is a ledger,
already marked for subtraction.
Canticle of the warhead, burst of light.
His shadow fixes to the wall,
refusing to follow him.

The earth said:
I have seen this before—
cities undone,
temples torn to the cornerstone.

Old men gnaw at the name of God.
Mothers wrap the dead
wordlessly in linen.
These are the waste places
where altars once consumed
lambs and turtledoves.

The earth said:
In me they rest.
In me there is no rest.

Night comes, black as the inside of a well.
And the moon over Gaza—
a white skull
passed from hand to hand
by indifferent angels.

Pip McGough
@manifest_gothic

Gaza

There are so many red lines being crossed. Intentionally. Makes it feel like hope is lost. Intentionally. Denying permission to let in any aid. In this day and age.

It should weigh on you. Deliberate starvation. It should enrage you. It should sit behind your eyelids as you sleep, in your teeth as you eat. Your soul as it is live-streamed.

The flattened hospitals, churches, homes, schools, tents. The men, women, children. Mums, dads, cousins, kids. Generations. What happened to never again? So many red lines it is hard to comprehend. This must end.

Lisa O'Hare

Blue Cloud

*North American Indians know everything about genocide! I had a
dream in which a Lakota Medicine Man could, fundamentally,
change the nature of things just by raising his hands. As ordinary
people, the simple act of raising our hands means we can't fight
each other.*

When Blue Cloud lifts his hands,
The clouds become blue
And the sky turns white.
It's a sign throughout the lands
That everything is going to be alright.
There'll be an end to all the fighting,
The human being's plight,
When Blue Cloud lifts his hands
He'll shift the veil of night.

Supplication! Celebration!
An invitation to the nature of things.
A simple action. Just a stance,
A chance to end all suffering!

No more rage, no more slavery,
No more cages ever again,
No more violence to women,
No more violence to women,
No more violence between men.
No more live like cannibals,
No more cruelty to animals,
No more cruelty to children,
No more wars between religions,
No more vanity! No more insanity!
No more Judaism vs Islam vs Christianity!
No worry no more.
No more war,
        No more war,
                No more war!

No Waterloo, No Dien Bien Phu,
No final breath on the Highway of Death,
No one to kill on Hamburger Hill,
No Huaihai, No Nagasaki,

No Bull Run, No Culloden,

No Gettysburg, No Stalingrad,
No running scared on the Streets of Baghdad,
No El Alamein, No Tiananmen,
No Bear River,
Gone, the great white indian giver
Forever and ever!
Never again Sand Creek,
No more massacre of the weak,
Blessed will be the meek
Who'll be forever free,
There'll be no more Wounded Knee,
        No more Wounded Knee,
            No more Wounded Knee,

Because Blue Cloud has raised his hands,
And the clouds have become blue
And the sky has turned white,
It's a sign to all the lands
That everything is going to be alright.
It's a sign to every woman,
It's a sign to every man,
To simply stand together
And simply raise your hands,
        Just raise your hands,
            Just raise your hands,
                Just raise your hands,

                And stop fighting!

                        Rowland Crowland

The Meaning of Words

My Dad's best friend was called Gordon Bennett.
No really, he was
and when I was young, I had no idea it was
a minced oath,
an abridged 'Gor blimey'.

They played squash together on Saturday mornings
in '70s short shorts at the local sports centre
while me and my brother swam in the pool
to give my mother a break.
They played squash as we swam and dived down, down
to where plasters and muck swirled against the tiles,
in a dead skin soup.
Our chlorine-blurred eyes searched for shipwrecks
beneath thrashing legs and muffled screams.
Our treasure trove, 10 pence for the vending machine.
It was more than enough.

I wonder what they talked about, my Dad and his friend
as they smashed hell out of a little rubber ball:
Politics? Romance? The price of fags?
My dad loved historical facts, he told me
that squash started in 18th century London prisons.
Makes sense.
A small space with high walls and a punctured ball.
Compressed men living compressed lives
all with different hang times,
coloured dots of data on someone's spreadsheet.

The original Gordon Bennett was either
an American dandy
or a biscuit maker from Pontefract.
No one seems to quite know.
My Gordon Bennett was my Dad's friend.
An unusual breed, he didn't have many.

As I got older, Gordon Bennett became shorthand for shock.
No longer my Dad's mate but a squashed euphemism.
And now I wonder about other words, how they are used to disguise
or confound.

And I wonder when the lie of fighting for a cause will finally be acknowledged as genocide.

And I wonder when the lie of fighting for a cause will finally be acknowledged as genocide.

Elizabeth Tunstall

The Whisper of Angels

What is so wrong with peace
that its story is so hard to tell,

like it was the whispered
rambling of angels
and not its own grace,
its own light.

I sift through the ruins
of another war where we never learnt,

watching its collapsed landscape
like the fallen truth
that we neglected to notice.

Clear away the rubble,
rebuild the past,
shorn of mortar and morality,
the humility of everything forgotten.

No people were heard
as they tried to tell us of the hurt,

just the hollow of misguided words
and the violence of each would-be God
who declares his surety, his rattle of certainty,
recasting holy books in twisted faith.

Only the ancient roads remember
why we walked this way,

to conquer other voices,
forget the sound of what we can be,
replaced now by the explosion of a bomb,
label it progress if you please.

Atrocity, our damaged humanity,
a wronging, whisper the angels unheard.
Night falls inside my head,

the shape of the moon is a bloody fist,
and my voice is silent, lost again,

no sound except for
the whisper of angels.

John Humphreys

Name Them

Fatima Mohammed Nour Reem Rafiq

The butchers are not done butchering yet
Because we let them
Because our leaders let them
Because our powerful men are giving them bombs

Aisha Malik Osama Hassan Nabil

In Gaza
Dirt is full of human flesh
Limbs hang from rubble
The air smells like death and pain and burning

Zain Mustafa Omar Younis Saba

The dead will not be saved
Bodies in white cloth held up against blue sky
With our bullets in them

Abdullah Wateen Farid Amira Siwar

The butchers are not done butchering yet
We make helmets and gloves to protect them
We give them artillery shells
And missiles too

Obeida Hind Salma Ashraf Habiba

They were looking for food
They were sleeping in their homes
They were playing outside

Mariam Taher Amal Ahmed Joud

Name them
Name them all

Malak Karim Sinam Aya Muna
Shout their names

The names of the children of Gaza
Flood the world
Broadcast into the cosmic
Start a tempest of names
Until the eardrums of the butchers and their providers explode

Pascale Collas

Our Poems Are Tears: for John Blight

- sorry we are, too, when a child dies;
but at the immolation of a race, who cries?

John Blight

I cry, John. I cry.
I see others cry too.
I see others cry, John, because this time,
we're all watching.
This time round, we can all see.
And we can't unsee it, John, it's in the palms of our hands
that's where we hold the scenes.
And we cry, John. We cry.
And I know you cried too,
your tears were those fourteen lines
because some poems are tears, John.
We are crying poems too.

Some of our tears are poems, some of our tears are songs,
some of our tears are sabotage, some of our tears are rage.
Some of our tears are paint,
sprayed across a canvas - or a jet
some of our tears are letters, some of our tears are prayers
some of our tears are placards, some of our tears are films
some of our tears are shame and hurt,
some of our tears are fists,
some of our tears are open arms, some of our tears are risks
some of our tears are revenge, some of our tears are peace
some of our tears are coins, for those who organise relief
some of our tears are guilt, John
because we failed to speak till now.

But we cry, John, we cry.
While we watch a people dying
we cry, John.

We are crying.

Anne Holloway

Australian poet John Blight's sonnet, *Death of a Whale*, was first published on
April 7th 1954

Legacy: for Gaza

Let no suns ever set or rise again
in the blaze of any beautiful burnt orange,
let us see from now on a ruby red sky,
strewn with the blood of so many -
of so many little ones.
Let their tiny souls hang forever more.

Let them hang from clouds that sob
into a screaming sea.
Let gentle whales whisper our pathetic woes
across all oceans,
let them shush the fullest of moons
and in doing let them calm the wise
and mightiest angry trees.

Let the fires of the mountains be forever fanned
and ready for the ashes
of the rise of no phoenix -
but of the death of

everything.

Lisa Moore

A Usual Day

Today I got up as usual
and made some tea
The house hadn't been bombed
I had muesli and toast for breakfast
I heard no explosions
I fed the cat
There was no sound of gunfire
I had a shower
There were no fallen
I got dressed
No one wept for the dead
I checked my phone
There were no desperate
calls from loved ones.
I looked out of the window
There were no tanks on the streets
I went out for a walk
No one made a dash for the border
The day was fine with blue skies
There was no drone of planes
only a gull gracefully arcing the air
No bombs, no bullets, no blitzkrieg
just a usual day.

Charles Pankhurst

Born Yesterday - A Version

They had never uttered a decibel.
Their voices trapped in concrete throats set to be born
as aliens amongst human beings

They had never stepped foot on sand
Castles built like government housing,
dwellings smashed into grey smithereens

They had never felt embarrassed
Kisses of life locked in public displays of affection
where heartbeats forcibly stop

They never got to be social
Zooming on the digital, swiping left
shopping for filters and vintage teeth

They had never been at the mercy of will
Freedom as forlorn as grey ash falls
from old garden rose and oud incense sticks.

They had never sat exams
That drip of sweat tasted bitter-sweet
as time ends without a five minute or 10 second warning

They had never seen the news
As good as it was, old news was scarce
And hand-me-downs were becoming more rare

They had never known nothing
Archives and context had been written into stars where seated
deities denied the universal trumping
of Acknowledgement.

Bea Udeh

Dream of Patriarchy #9

There is a man in my house who throws his weight around, energetically and violently, who does not leave until every precious thing is broken, the stereo busted and the pans scraped to their chemical core. His fingers leave prints all over the walls, the furniture, all over us. When he is here I do not sleep and when he leaves I sleep in fear of his return.

There are men here who abuse everybody I know and, as we try again and again to make this known, onlookers form a playground jury, making a game of who to believe. I dream of these men, these snakes, who hide behind trees if looked at directly, or turn to cruel butterflies, dazzling the eyes.

The jury decorate themselves with newsprint, following their juggler, who follows the band, who follow the butterflies; and the circus parades through the forest, picking up the lost-in-the-woods, the new and precious babes, the warped and jaded ex-sinners. They whirl their streamers around me until I am bound fast to this tree and I want to warn them but the band are so loud and I only watch as the wandering vulnerable dance into danger, following the butterflies.

I share this dream with many others
and from this dream, we cannot wake.

umbilica

128

One of a Kind City

On the map, there is a tiny dot,
Called Gaza —
It looks like any other spot,
But everything there is different.
The people are free:
To die beneath the rubble,
Or live behind bars.
The children may:
Starve in silence,
Or vanish in the blast.
The elderly can:
Mourn their lost days,
Or mourn the wiped names
Of those they love.
In Gaza, the people are free —
But only to die
In today's world
Of human rights.

Ahmed F Khaleel

Words of War

We yearn for peace
but grudgingly settle for those sanitised
words of war, 'collateral damage.'
A phrase deemed fit for our consumption.
We quickly forget the crippled communities
the homes that have become blasted mausoleums.
Our eyes shielded from hideous mutilation
subjugation and brutal annihilation
ethnic cleansing and genocide.
We yearn for peace but choose to look away
shaking our heads, we grudgingly accept
the words of war, 'collateral damage.'

Graham Lowe

The Moral High Ground

The quiet gravel road echoes a peace
that some take for granted
while others pray,
'there is no god but God',
forced to bend
to the will of those playing God.
Still others bend over ghostly white sheet
perhaps in doubt of the very existence of God.
The warlords compete for the high ground, but to no avail.
For only a dove
on a telephone wire
overlooking a quiet gravel road
                              can boast such a vantage point.

Alida

Comit This To Memory

Pass along your knowledge.
Commit everything to memory.
When savages come to town
as they always do
they will burn down
libraries
books.
No army is moral.
Sabra
Shatila
exhibits
in a museum I create at will
when I shut my eyes.

Haroon Khan

This is the Key to My House

This is the key to my house
Worn by my pocket and my hand
Through the churning of the century
No turning of a key.
This is the key to my home
Hung on the door many yesterdays ago
Forced by a war to roam
From the village of my youth
A reminder of the truth
Of my home
This is the key to my house
Now I can see the door
But time has changed the name
The family's not the same
The key may never turn again
This is the key to my house
Why do I hold it in my hand?
The past has disappeared
With the mourning of the years
All lost in the seas of time
My house looks out to me saying,
Come and set me free!
Plant the roses by the stair,
Light the fireplace and share
All the stories that you know with me
But I turn and look away
Knowing I may never stay
In the home where I would be
Once again.
This is the key to my house

Karen Melander Magoon

Letter from Plumstead Jail

What's most significant about sitting or lying in a police cell in South East London, is how civilised it is. Maybe this has something to do with me being a white British male but I can't help but think about Palestinian children being detained in an Israeli hell hole by those who viscerally despise you and process you in a language you don't understand and without a responsible adult there.

I wasn't connecting the disparate situations emotionally, I was consumed with acclimatising to a situation completely alien to me — in a cell on my own, with no personal belongings or devices to interact with. Cut off from the outside world with no means of exiting except at the convenience of my captors. It was odd being referred to as a prisoner as the police were communicating from the police van while transporting me to the station. It was the strangeness that occupied my mind, relying on my instincts and not any past experience.

Breaking the law

That I hadn't crossed any ethical line didn't evoke any sense of injustice on my part. If anything it was a comfort, as I didn't have to suppress my unrelenting sense of guilt that normally accompanies even the mildest rebuke or correction.

I'd taken part in a protest against the proscription of Palestine Action, displaying my own poster which detailed my support of said organisation. Initially, I was disturbed by the arrest of fellow protesters nearby, especially those who seemed least deserving of being manhandled by the police. However, as my time drew near I dialled down my sense of shock, pity and disapproval.

I did almost nothing

Everyone holding up their sign had done so fully aware that they were breaking the law and likely to be arrested, and the police actions were largely mechanical. I've since learned of police being heavy-handed and of some protesters being very anxious and scared. I surprised myself how calm I was and am only now appreciating the gravity of the situation. It felt like a game with everyone playing their part. It mostly went to script and hardly matters now. What does matter is what we were protesting for.

Being processed

We'd been advised to take a book with us as time in the cell can drag and be disorienting. My time in the police cell was relatively short and broken up by two calls (one from my solicitors and one from prison support), having my fingerprints taken along with mug shots and having a cup of tea with biscuits. I wasn't there any longer than seven hours and slept most of the time, so a book wasn't necessary.

The cell was clean and it had a flushable toilet. There was a mattress and mattress-like pillow and I was given two blankets. Apparently I could have asked for the lights to be turned down but I managed to sleep, regardless. As I drifted off to sleep I went through imaginary conversations with my captors but quickly coming back to reality. This was me, on my own and I wasn't in control.

If I could condense my experience to a few words I would have to say "I did almost nothing". Yes, I'd prepared for the demo, for the potential arrest and for minimising any risk but I was largely following a script. Yet, as I've subtitled this article, it was mostly about **turning up**.

...that's what it's all about

Many are the discussions about the significance of our actions. For those now remanded in prison yet without charge it was the lack of impact their activism was having that stirred them into positive direct action. The only actions left to them were destructive ones. The Government would only listen when its toys were taken away. They felt no guilt in causing millions of pounds worth of damage to an arms company; the only guilt they felt came from not doing enough.

Yet we should resist creating a hierarchy of activism. Rather we should consider why we do what we do, what do we believe it will achieve and do we think we have achieved our objective. Sometimes the objective is quite abstract and consists of little more than showing support. There is no need to compare what we do against what others do yet it's still important to understand some basic principles when it comes to being part of a movement.

An example

If £1,000 was being raised by 10 donors giving £100 each, anyone pulling out would impact the fund by £100. If the same sum was being contributed by 1,000 donors the impact would be inconsequential should anyone fail to donate. Consequently anyone not contributing need feel no guilt but could be proud to contribute their pound. Similarly it's good to march for Palestine but not worth agonising over not being able to when it's a numbers game.

What comes next?
I've not yet been charged. Whatever happens as a consequence of being arrested, I feel I've crossed a Rubicon. I've stepped out of my existing comfort zone and challenged my preconceptions. The mountains and valleys of my past have been truncated and filled in respectively.

We all need to recognise how we live in our own cells with constraints not only created by the walls we build but also by being ignorant of who is the key holder and what power is invested in them. We need to better understand the direct and indirect connections between what we do and what we can realistically achieve.

I've been in the company of serial offenders, talking about their adventures and they're remarkably ordinary — none pretending to be anything other than concerned citizens. What's particularly significant is not what they've done but that they turned up and they will continue to turn out.

Palestine Action largely targeted Elbit Systems, an Israeli arms company with factories in the UK. They've successfully closed various factories down and cost the company millions of pounds in revenue and orders. The Filton 18 have already spent more than a year in remand with their trial still many months off. They are being treated shoddily including having basic privileges denied and other inmates being warned not to associate with them.

Their families have also been harassed and had their houses raided. The Government is clearly making an example of them as a warning not to challenge the seat of power. The protest held on 6th September 2025 aimed to overwhelm the Metropolitan police in order to demonstrate that proscribing Palestine Action is bad law, futile and unworkable.

In a stroke of irony, it was disclosed on September 6th that the Elbit factory at Filton in Bristol has closed down. Around 900 protesters were arrested by police officers brought in from all over the country.

Chris Price

Contributors

Contributors to this anthology come from around the globe, and have all kinds of life and work experience. Some are professional writers, or academics, some have been published many times before, and others have picked up a pen to contribute specifically to this book. My job as an editor has been to ensure that the voice of each writer has been heard as they intended, any edits have been 'light touch' and the views of each individual writer are their own. I have also chosen to leave US spellings as they are, rather than standardising to UK spellings, likewise punctuation is as each author prefers. We have added some notes for context if we thought it might help or be of interest. Some have chosen to share notes about themselves and others prefer to be credited by name alone.

Abigail Hutchison - @_abigail_writes_
Nottingham born, Manchester based poet, young people's workshop facilitator.

Ahmed F Khaleel
Lecturer in Arabic (language, literature & culture), Arabic module convenor (LFA & YLE), Impact and Engagement officer (ESRC project), Sanctuary Expert, Muslim community representative, Dept of Language & Linguistic Science, Chair of York City of Sanctuary, York Hate Crime Partnership member.

Alexandra Jorg
Writer, actress, and performing arts teacher who works at the edge of memory, migration, and resistance, using poetry and performance to confront silence, grief, and the violence that shapes our bodies and histories.

Alida - @your_editing_retreat
Upcycled academic editor & amateur poet.

Ambrose Musiyiwa
Poet, journalist with a background in the intersection between activism, migration and community action. He coordinates Journeys in Translation, an international, volunteer-driven initiative that is translating *Over Land, Over Sea: Poems for those seeking refuge* (Five Leaves Publications, 2015) into other languages, and is on the editorial board of the Africa Migration Report Poetry Anthology Series.

Amelia Harker
English for Academic Purposes Lecturer at the University of Edinburgh, second generation Palestinian living in the diaspora, mother who weeps with the mothers in Gaza, academic advocating for decolonisation.

Anastasia Christou
Professor of Sociology and Social Justice School of Law and Social Sciences, Middlesex University.

Andy Winters
Children's author. Restorative Justice practitioner. Co-founder of Resource Creatives www.resourcecreatives.co.uk

Anna Greensted-Payne
Shift Bristol Permaculture student.

Anne Holloway - @webepoets - @bigwhiteshed
Poet based in Morecambe, UK. Founding editor at Big White Shed. Story Fellow, StoryArcs, Bath Spa University. Surviving by Storytelling lead, Institute of Mental Health, Nottingham.
We are all poets.

Bea Udeh
Bea believes that inclusivity is much harder to achieve than inclusion. So she spends her time building relationships that bring the historical context into her work, her words and your understanding of the world.

Bill Pook
Performance poet and musician/singer/songwriter.

Breffní Lennon
Research Fellow at the Sustainability Institute, University College, Cork.

Calliope - @calliopemermuse

An ethereal poet, performer, and passionate activist; advocating for radical hope and decolonising imagination. Bridging activism, creativity, and healing. You can find *Beating Hearts Break Ribs* online @calliopemermuse and Erin James's Sounds of the Revolution, Live Archive: https://new.express.adobe.com/webpage/M0RuJdy9BrsoV

Casey Bailey

Writer, performer and educator from Nechells, Birmingham. He was Birmingham Poet Laureate 2020-2022

Cathal Mac Thréinfhir

Lives on the mid-west coast of Ireland, and is currently working on his first poetry collection.

Catherine Marina - @cathmarina

Lives and works in Lancashire and Cumbria. She has had short fiction and poetry published in anthologies and online. She came to poetry late after having a family and currently works in hospitality, from which she is endlessly inspired.

Cathy Symes

Writer and poet living in Nottingham.

Charles Josefson

Charles Pankhurst

Originally a Man of Kent, now lives in Morecambe and sometimes performs his poetry and short stories in the area. His work has appeared in several magazines and he won his first poetry competition in 2021. He has an MA in Creative Writing.

Chris Price

Morecambe based musician and writer.

Claire Griffel

Read about her online: ClaireGriffel.com and ImagineSenegal.com

Daron Carey - fb.me/daroncareypoet

Derbyshire based poet.

Deb Michel

Dee Allen

African-Italian performance poet based in Oakland, California U.S.A. Active on creative writing & Spoken Word since the early 1990s. Author of 10 books—*Boneyard, Unwritten Law, Stormwater, Skeletal Black, Elohi Unitsi, Rusty Gallows: Passages Against Hate, Plans, Crimson Stain, Discovery* and his newest, *The Mansion*—and 82 anthology appearances under his figurative belt so far.

Drew Milne

Judith E Wilson Professor of Poetics, Faculty of English, University of Cambridge. His collected poems, *In Darkest Capital* were published by Carcanet in 2017.

Edward Foreman @foreman_eddy

Washington, DC native, who goes by the poet name Ed Poetastic because he wants to make people's lives extra fantastic. Has been writing poetry for eight years, putting in extra thought and cheer. A regular at Nuyorican, Barbwire, Antics, The Mitch Salon, Phynnecabulary, Time to Arrive, The Word is Write, Moist Mondays, Unmesh Life Open Mic, Tokyo Kotoba, and many more!

Elizabeth Tunstall

Poet, living in Birmingham.

Fran Sani

UK-based Italian writer, researcher, and trade unionist. With a background as a playwright and performer, he is currently developing applied theatre projects on labour rights advocacy and antiracism in partnerships with different educational charities and trade unions from across the UK. His poetry has appeared, among others, in *Welcome to Britain: An Anthology of Poems and Short Fiction* (Civic Leicester), as an artistic contribution to the Journal of Critical Studies on Security, in Parcham Online, and in *Dimly Writ*. You can find Fran's Substack blog at: https://substack.com/@fransani

Gail Webb - @poetry_cocktail

Creative writing facilitator at Maggie's Centre, Nottingham. Shortlisted for Bridport Poetry Prize 2024, HIghly Commended at Verve Poetry Festival 2025.

Gerald Kells

Poet, writer and environmentalist from Walsall, England. His poems and stories have been published in a number of anthologies and his collection *LI - 51 Poems* is available from Lulu Publishing. His involvement in the *PoArtry Project* in Stourbridge led to the publication of *Nine Etchings* with Fran Wilde. His young teen novel, *The Net Mender's Son*, is available as an e-book. He has won several poetry slams and you can also find some of his poems on Soundcloud and YouTube.

Graham Lowe

Lancaster based artist and art tutor.

Gregory Woods

Poet with Carcanet Press and a queer cultural historian with Yale University Press.

Haroon Khan - @harooncreates

South London based author, poet, performer and educator. Autistism and ADHD champion.

Hazel Warren - @hazeleypoos

Member of DIY Poets and Papercranes collectives (Nottingham UK). Hazel's debut collection *To See the Moon* (2019) is available from Big White Shed, her work has also appeared online and in various anthologies.

Ian Chapman

Ian holds a PhD in Creative Writing from Lancaster University. His work has appeared in *Dream Catcher, Allegro, Streetcake* and others. He lives on the edge of the English Lake District where he enjoys hillwalking, performing poetry and drumming with a local samba band.

Jane Flint Bridgewater

Writing in retirement from cardiology practice in West Midlands, UK. Twin tragedies in Gaza have struck home for me as a mother of twins, and compiling my own collection of poems around multiple birth. Communicating science through poetry in *Consilience* and interlacing words with harp music have also become important strands.

Jane Wignall

Creative. Co-founder of Resource Creatives.
www.resourcecreatives.co.uk

Jerri Daboo
Has worked as an actress, director, and writer. She is currently Professor of Performance at University of Exeter, UK.

Jess Gibson - @jagged.little.jellybean
Poet, Nottingham, UK.

Jim Lupton
Writer of fiction, drama and poetry. Co-founder of The Nib Crib writers' collective, Morecambe, UK.

John D Kelly
Works and lives in Co. Fermanagh. His work has been widely published. His first collection, *The Loss of Yellowhammers* was published by Summer Palace Press in 2020. His second collection *About Blood* was published by Revival Press in May 2025.

John P Hindle
In 2023 he launched his first poetry pamphlet alongside an exhibition of abstract art, which is available in libraries in the UK as well as New Zealand and New York. He has been doing some work with universities recently, informing the social consciousness evident in his writing. His poetry is frequently inspired by visual art, particularly through collaborations with artists.

John Humphreys
Nottingham based poet.

Kaia Allen-Bevan - she/her @kaia.ab
Award winning founder of Youth TheGap CIC, a TEDx speaker described as 'making a Global impact,' she has curated TEDx Brighton 2022, amplifying youth voices and global awareness. Self-taught, multi-medium artist who has had her work featured in CasildART's "EmpowerHER" exhibition (2024), Osprey's Black History Month 2022 National Installation and Playing The Race Card's Exhibtion "Black Joy" (2024) Her poetry has been widely published in magazines and journals. She translates her activism into joyful yet political pieces that call for community healing and cohesion.

Karen Melander Magoon
San Francisco based poet who writes often about nature and social justice. You can find out more about her at www.karenmm.com

Lahraeb Munir - @poetry4pal
Poet.

Laura Grevel
Originally from the USA, Laura has lived in Europe 25 years. Her writings are eclectic, tackling the immigrant experience, human rights, narratives and nature. Her work has been published widely, in anthologies, literary journals and online publications. She is an active member of the international online poetry community and is currently putting together her debut collection on the theme of immigration. You can view her poetry performances on her YouTube channel, including a collaborative video called *'Girl Walking Across Europe'* by Poets for Refugees, created as an act of welcome.

Lennart Lundh
Great-grandparent. Poet, photographer, historian, and short-fictionist. His work has appeared internationally since 1965.

Lisa Moore - @mooretrouble1
Actor, writer, educator and poet. Author of *and she dances...* (Big White Shed).

Lisa O'Hare - @lisaoharepoet
Poet.

Lytisha Tunbridge - @lytishat
Nottingham based, poet, performer, editor, VR content creator, workshop facilitator, event host, and co-creator of Women Say Stuff - you can find out more on her website
https://lytishapoet.co.uk

Magdalena Szczerba
Polish born immigrant who has found a safe space and home in England for 18 years now. An artist at heart, and a healer with a purpose to defend the weak, be a voice for the voiceless and bring sight for the blind. Fluently speaking the language of love to those who need it most.

Marett Troostwyk
Person Centred Therapist and artist.

Marijn Nieuwenhuis
A Human Geographer at Durham University. His work is driven by a curiosity for conceptual art, disregarded things, and elemental experiments. He has written on holes, weather, air, breathing, skin, dust, sand, and fire.

Mary Loveday
Researcher, lecturer, writer and editor, and creative practitioner in Arts & Ecology; works as a Lecturer in Design Theory at Sunderland University, and pursues research in design, ecology, performance, and nostalgia.

Marzia D'Amico - @atamarzia
Academic researcher, poet, and translator. They are author of *Ragazz* Laser* (Zona, 2025) and the poetic artefact *Liricologismo* (Zacinto, 2023). In addition to their scholarly work and cultural contributions, their multilingual poetry has appeared in a range of international print and online journals, and they have performed at various international events and poetry festivals. They translate prose and non-fiction from English, and poetry between English and Italian. Together with two comrades, they curate the monthly transfeminist newsletter *Ghinea* and serve as editor of the column *Autopoetica* for Argonline.

Meher Pestonji -@meherpestonji
Writer of fiction, drama and poetry.

Michael Durack
Lives in Co. Tipperary, Ireland. He is the author of a memoir in prose and poems, Saved to Memory: *Lost to View* (2016) and three poetry collections, *Where It Began* (2017), *Flip Sides* (2020) and *This Deluge of Words* (2023) published by Revival Press.

Molly Bland @molly.bland
Illustrator, designer and creative facilitator based on West Street, Morecambe.

Naomi L.A 'Baudelaire' Smith
Systems Healer, Decolonial Strategist, Architect of Liberation at Black and Gold Education, DIE4ART Creative Consultant.

N. Chamchoun

Nicholas Manganas

Senior lecturer in International Studies and Global Sciences, School of International Studies and Education, University of Technology Sydney.

Nico Edwards - @nicosananes.bsky.social

Doctoral researcher, anti-militarist organiser and co-founder of the annual Global Week of Action for Peace and Climate Justice. Based in London.

Önder Çakırtaş

Academic, writer, and poet, whose work bridges the realms of literature and theatre. Specializing in English literature and contemporary theatre, he has developed a particular expertise in modern political theatre, as well as the representation of ethnic, racial, and disability narratives on stage. Beyond his academic contributions, Önder shares insights, reflections, and resources with a wider audience through his online presence at ondercakirtas.com, engaging readers and theatre enthusiasts alike with his unique perspective on literature and performance.

Pascale Collas

Apprentice poet, mother, environmentalist, feminist, living in Ottawa. Hoping to change the world one poem at a time.

Pip McGough - @manifest_gothic

Nottingham-based lawyer and writer.

Reem Farajallah

Arab-British Palestinian, born in Gaza, she carries stories across borders between the UAE and the UK. A mother, counsellor, and clinical supervisor with a love for words, once a translator and teacher, she now walks with others through their inner landscapes, finding her own peace in books and nature's paths.

Rena Fleming

Poet, living in Ireland. Author of two chapbooks, *Somebody and Nobody,* and *Spidéal*.

Richard Spisak

An artist, a poet, a hermit, a storyteller, a temporary earthling.

Richerprioritys - @richerpriority

Richer Priority is a Nottingham-based spoken word poet and former rapper. His poetry captures lived experiences and celebrates the essence of hip hop.

Rosemary Drescher

Has embraced her vocation as a poet since retiring from biomedical research administration. She was born in Sydney, grew up in Kiribati, Fiji and the UK and lived for over 20 years in Germany. Her exposure to different languages in childhood, at school and university shaped her love of poetry. Since the 1990s she has published a body of work in journals and anthologies and has read at events and festivals. She is the Lancaster Stanza rep and most recently joint winner of the Morecambe Poetry Festival Competition LA3/LA4 prize.

Rowland Crowland

Manchester born poet living in Morecambe. AKA The Goblin Poet. His books include *Thief, Outcast* (both published by Big White Shed) *Word Dancing,* and *Beggars.*

Sarah Attfield

Teaches creative writing at the University of Technology, Sydney Australia. She is the co-editor of the *Journal of Working-Class Studies.*

Sarah Attwell

Actor, & Writer who studied at Salford University. A regular on the spoken word scene, she has appeared across Manchester guesting for many and being commissioned for specific works.

Satkirti Sinha

Graduate Teaching Assistant and PhD researcher in the Performing Arts Department at DMU University. Satkirti's areas of expertise are Performance Theory, Folk Culture, Dalit Theology, Performance Politics, Feminist Theory, Postcolonial Theory, and Sexual Politics.

Serena B. Slack-Robins
Has worked in theatre for 28 years, teaches at 'The Guildhall School of Music & Drama' as an acting tutor and at an adult community college as an English and Creative Writing lecturer. She is a poet, a children's book author and illustrator. She is a PhD candidate, researching: 'British Muslim Communities' Engagement with Theatre,' in collaboration with Khayaal Theatre Company, Manchester Metropolitan University, and is funded by the NWCDTP.

Syra Shakir
Associate Professor in Learning and Teaching and Strategic Lead on Race Equity at Leeds Trinity University. She works on embedding race equity in the curriculum, decolonisation, anti-racist pedagogy, and co-creation with students to build belonging.

Teo Eve
Author of *The Ox House* and *I Imagine An Image*.

Tess Hurson

Trevor Wright
Trainer and consultant specialising in neurodiversity, a member of Nottingham's DIY Poets and of the Social Model Writers group. He established the Beyond the Spectrum creative writing project for autistic people with Writing East Midlands (beyondthespectrum.uk), is a Trustee of the Nottingham Unesco City of Literature and a Fellow of the Royal Society of Arts. Trevor is the author of two Big White Shed poetry collections, *Outsider Heart* and *Salt Flow*.

Turtle - @turtlepoetryinsta
Notts-based poet interested in Class and Language.

umbilica
Nottingham & Derby-based queer poet, songcrafter & musician; plays in dream-pop band *Grawl!x*. Spoken word performer with GOBS collective. Chapbooks include *PleasureLand* (2021) and *And They Say That We Are Strange* (forthcoming in 2025), published by Big White Shed. Works with university students by day; lives with one beloved partner and one belligerent cat.

William Patrick
Irish teacher and editor horrified by the crisis in Gaza.

Helping to get the stories out...

Big White Shed, founded in 2015, is a not-for-profit indie publisher, expert in peer publishing, offering support with writing and editing as well as mentoring - a place to seek advice and tools, trade expertise and ideas. All fees paid to Big White Shed for projects and services are passed directly to our editors, designers, proof readers, artists etc...

Want to support poets in Gaza, buy their books and read their stories? *Gaza Poets Society* is a Gaza-based literary organisation dedicated to promoting the work of emerging artists and poets in the Gaza Strip. Through their publications and initiatives, they act as a conduit for Gazan poets to connect with the international literary community. https://www.gazapoets.org/

If you'd like to learn more about Palestine, check out *Makan*, they are an independent, non-partisan organisation dedicated to intersectional learning. They provide transformative education aimed at strengthening the movement for Palestinian liberation, contextualising Palestine within the broader framework of social justice and global liberation movements. https://www.makan.org.uk/

If you'd like to learn more about how Jews are supporting Palestinians (UK organisations) you can find out more through *Jewish Network for Palestine* and *Jews for Justice for Palestinians*. www.jewishnetworkforpalestine.uk www.jfjfp.com